Longman Handbooks for Language Teachers

Longman Handbooks for Language Teachers
Consultant Editors: Neville Grant and Jeremy Harmer

Margaret Allan

Teaching English with Video

Longman

Longman Group Limited,
Longman House, Burnt Mill, Harlow,
Essex CM20 2JE, England
and Associated Companies throughout the world

First published 1985
ISBN 0 582 74616 7

BRITISH LIBRARY CATALOGUING IN PUBLICATION DATA
Allan, Margaret
Teaching English with video. — (Longman
handbooks for language teachers)
1. English language — Study and teaching —
Foreign speakers 2. English language — Study and
teaching — Audio-visual instruction 3. Video tapes
in education
I. Title
428.2′4′078 PE1128.42
ISBN 0-582-74616-7

Set in 10/12pt Times, MCS
Printed in Great Britain
by The Bath Press, Avon

ACKNOWLEDGEMENTS

We are grateful to the following for permission to reproduce copyright
material:

British Broadcasting Corporation for extracts from *Television English* (c) BBC & The British
Council (1985); Centre for Information on Language Teaching and Research and The British
Council for extracts from *Language Teaching Library Bibliography B13* (June 1984) pub jointly
by CILT & The British Council; Free University of Berlin for extracts from pp 57-59,133 'An
Intensive Theme-Orientated Course in Advanced English for First-Semester German University
Students of Diverse Subject Studies' by J Schwartz, v Bevan & S Lasche (Freie Universitat
Berlin, Modellversuch Fremdsprachenorientierte Studieneingangsphase, Schrift-enreihe, Heft 6)
Copyright 'Fremdsprachenorientierte Studieneingangsphase' Modellversuch des Bundes und des
Landes Berlin; Macmillan, London and Basingstoke for extracts from pp 53-55, 69, 57-60
Video English (VC1 & VC8) British Council; Oxford University Press for a table from the
article 'Viewing Comprehension in the EFL Classroom' by Margaret Allan p 22 *English
Language Teaching Journal* Vol 38/1 (Jan 1984) pub OUP & The British Council; Thames
Television International for extracts from pp 23,24,29 Episode 1 worksheets 7,8,10 *The John
Smith Show*, p 23 worksheet 6 *SWALK*, p 19 worksheet 2 *Middle English*.

We are grateful to the following for permission to reproduce copyright photographs:

Australian Tourist Commission for page 26; BBC Copyright Photograph for page 24; 'Follow
Me to San Francisco' © BBC English by Radio and Television 1985 for page 56; Dundee
College of Education for page viii (right); 'Family Affair Study Guide' by Brian Abbs and
Ingrid Freebairn for page 54; Independent Television News Limited for page 27; Kelloggs
Limited for page 30; Rank Strand Limited for page 12 (right); © 1985 Walt Disney
Productions for page 29.
All other photographs were taken by the Longman Photographic Unit.

Contents

Author's acknowledgements

This book has grown out of my work in the British Council and many of the ideas in it are those of colleagues I have worked with in Iran and London. I also owe a lot to the many groups of teachers I have been fortunate enough to meet and work with around the world. I have particularly drawn on ideas developed in workshops I ran with teachers of the Anglo-Brazilian Culturas in 1984. My special thanks to three special friends and colleagues: to Jane Willis who started the whole thing off and worked on the first outline with me, to John McGovern whose work on the initial design of Video English helped me shape my ideas about video for the classroom and to Dave Willis who commented on an early draft and who inspires us all.

I would also like to acknowledge two books which were of particular help to me, *Interactive Video* by Eric Parsloe for the factual information on videodisc systems and CILT's *UK Sources of Computer Software for Modern Languages* for the list of software sources.

Introduction

What is video?

The word 'video' can mean different things to different people:

'I've got a video at home.'
'Our school's got video.'
'Video is an important tool in management training.'

For most people the first statement would mean a video recorder. That is a machine which can be linked to the television set to record TV programmes as they are broadcast. This is called recording 'off-air'. The recorded programme is then played back through the television set.

'Video' in management training most probably means a video camera which plugs into a video recorder and records onto videotape. This recording can then be played back through a TV set in the same way as a recorded TV programme.

'Our school has video' might mean several things. If it is true in your case, what does it mean to you? These are some of the possibilities:

A videocassette recorder linked to a television set

Individual viewing booths in the library

A portable one-camera system

A small recording studio

*The recording studio
control room*

An editing suite

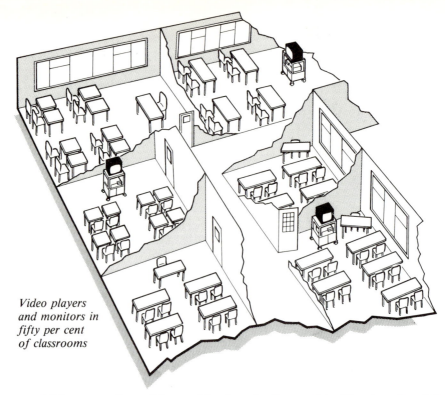

*Video players
and monitors in
fifty per cent
of classrooms*

This range of possible combinations is discussed in Chapters 1 and 2. The basic distinction to be made is between systems which include a camera and those which do not. The first allows you to make your own materials, the second restricts you to the use of material made by other people.

In what learning situations can video be used?

This book is concerned with the uses of video in language learning and teaching. In this field video playback systems are now being used as an aid by the teacher in the classroom, by the learner working at home or in the library and in the training of teachers. Systems with cameras are most commonly associated with teacher training but they are also being used in some classrooms with and by language learners. Teachers also use them to produce their own teaching materials.

How this book is organised

Each of these applications of video in language teaching is dealt with in this book with the main emphasis on video playback in the classroom. Part 1 describes *what* there is in terms of hardware — the equipment — and software — the materials. Part 2 then moves on to *how* these can be used, before tackling the question *why* video might be used in a language programme. This part includes a chapter on using a camera in the classroom. Part 3 looks at the roles of video playback and of the video camera in a teacher-training programme. Part 4 is about self-access by the learner to video materials and includes a discussion of interactive video. This part concludes with a chapter on another form of self-access: the use of a camera by teachers who wish to produce their own materials.

1

A guide
to video playback systems

**The basic
hardware**

Video and audio signals can be recorded onto videotape. This may be stored on open spools and played back on a videotape player or recorder. The recorders are referred to as VTRs.

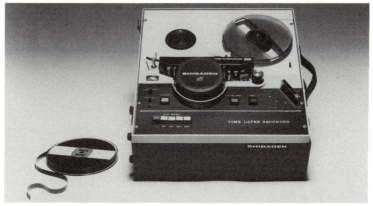

*A videotape
recorder (VTR)*

Alternatively the tape may be boxed in a cassette and then requires a videocassette player or recorder for playback. The recorders are referred to as VCRs.

*A videocassette
recorder (VCR)*

Video and audio signals can also be recorded onto videodisc. In this case playback is on a videodisc player or recorder. For the time being only videodisc players are on the market, although recorders are on their way.

A videodisc player

The playback machine reads the video and audio signals recorded on the tape or disc and these are carried to a monitor which reproduces the picture and the sound.

The videoplayer is linked to a monitor

The machine referred to as a monitor may be one of two types:

(a) A television receiver/monitor   This is a television set which has the capacity to accept video signals in addition to receiving broadcast television signals. If you want to record off-air you may need this type of set.

(b) A monitor   This receives audio and video signals from a video player but is not designed to receive broadcast television signals, so will not function as a television set and cannot be used for off-air recording.

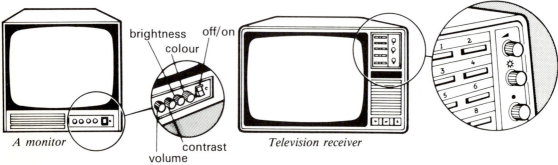

A monitor   *Television receiver*

Hardware choices   The first choice - between tape, cassette or disc - may seem easy at the moment because videocassette is so clearly in the lead. In Britain booming domestic sales of videocassette machines have brought the prices down and made them more attractive to institutions. Compared to open-reel tape machines they are also easier to load and store and provide better protection for the tape.

There is still doubt about domestic sales of videodisc but the manufacturers of videodisc systems in Britain have now begun to take note of the interest they attract in the world of education and training. Experimental work is going on in the production of educational software for videodisc. It is too early to be sure whether this new technology will establish itself in our schools but, if you are investigating the potential of video in an institution, you should certainly know what videodisc is capable of.

Videodisc compared to videocassette   A videodisc player can be connected up to a monitor or television set in the same way as a videocassette player. You could use the same monitor for either, so it is quite conceivable that institutions would in the future include both among their video equipment. These are the major areas of difference between the two:

(a) Storage of information

A videodisc has the capacity to store both still and moving pictures. Depending on the system, a disc can contain from thirty to sixty minutes' of moving pictures on each side. It stores still pictures in a way that is very economical of space and can store about 54,000 still pictures per side (depending on the system). This is the equivalent of 54,000 pages, so you could put the whole of the *Longman Dictionary of Contemporary English* and more on one side of a disc. You could also have a 'moving' dictionary, with a mixture of text, slides and moving film. The technology is being developed to allow for the sound to continue even when the picture is 'frozen' on the screen. Disc is therefore much more versatile than videotape for storing and playing back sound, moving pictures, still pictures, and all kinds of data.

(b) Access

A videodisc player works on the same principle as a record player in that an arm moves back and forth across the disc. You can move from the beginning of a disc to the end in about five seconds. The machine will also find a precise point in a programme with absolute accuracy every time. Compared to videotape players which move the tape past a head in a linear way, this speed of access combined with random access to any point in a programme gives videodisc much greater flexibility.

(c) Quality of picture and sound

The reproduction of both pictures and sound is superior on videodisc. With 'freeze frame', that is when the picture is frozen on the screen, the picture is steady and clear. With one system, the disc is read by a laser beam which does not touch the surface so it cannot be damaged. Freeze frame is also possible with most videocassette machines but the picture is often unstable and the tape can be damaged if it is stopped too often at the same point.

(d) Link-up to computer

This is possible with both disc and cassette machines, and is discussed in Chapter 10 (see section on Interactive Video). The advantages of disc in the storage of information and in speed of access to any part make it the more flexible combination, with a wider range of possible uses.

(e) Record facility

You cannot record onto the videodisc machines currently on the market. This is a major disadvantage for home users where the most common use of videocassette machines is to record off-air. It would therefore also be a disadvantage in institutions which use off-air material, as many language schools in English-speaking countries do. However there are videodisc recorders around and presumably this technology will develop if there is a demand for it.

Videodisc systems

Videodisc technology is still evolving and different systems are competing in a market which is still uncertain. We will look briefly at some of the systems currently on offer. Each system is incompatible with the others.

(a) Reflective optical discs

These are known as laser discs because the signal is read by a laser beam which decodes variations in reflected light imprinted on the disc. There is therefore no physical contact between the surface of the disc and the reading device. There are two types of disc within this system:

(i) 'Active Play' discs (CAV: Constant Angular Velocity)   The essential property of these for education is that one revolution of the disc produces one frame of video at any point on the disc. This means that any single frame can be found quickly and accurately and it can be held on the screen for as long as you like without damaging the disc. Still pictures in freeze frame are clear and sharply defined. It is also possible to 'step frame', that is to move forward or back one frame at a time, with absolute clarity. The disc revolves at a constant speed, holds 54,000 frames per side, and offers about thirty minutes of straight playing time on each side. The speed of access combined with precision of access to any part of the disc makes it an important development for educational users of video.

(ii) 'Long Play' discs (CLV: Constant Linear Velocity)   The frames on these discs are assigned differently and they do not play at constant speed. Playing time is longer - about one hour of straight playing time per side - but random access is less accurate. This version is intended for continuous play and is most suitable for entertainment viewing.

(b) Capacitance discs

Capacitance systems store and read audio and video signals by electrical means. An electrode-bearing stylus is used to read the signals and is in contact with the surface of the disc. There are two capacitance systems:

(i) 'SelectaVision' (CED: Capacitance Electronic Disc)   This uses a shallow groove to direct the stylus and is called the 'grooved' capacitance disc. It plays back four frames on each revolution of the disc so you cannot freeze the frame at any point you choose. It offers about one hour's straight playing time per side. This system is aimed at the home entertainment market.

(ii) VHD: Very High Density (The grooveless capacitance disc)   This system plays back two frames per revolution and holds 45,000 still frames. Continuous play is about one hour per side. With two frames for every revolution, the picture is not absolutely steady in freeze frame unless the material has been pre-recorded for this. However random access is fast and accurate and VHD is the main rival on the British market to the Active Play laser disc for education and training uses. Both systems have two audio tracks and VHD has the added capacity to play back digitally recorded sound from Audio High Density (AHD) discs (with the addition of a special decoder).

Videocassette systems

As I have said, videocassette systems currently dominate the domestic and the institutional market. The main systems in use in schools and colleges are VHS, Betamax and U-matic. VHS and Betamax use tape which is half an inch wide, while U-matic uses three-quarter inch tape. The wider tape gives better quality reproduction and the machines are very robust - an important consideration for the classroom. They are however considerably more expensive.

New versions of each format appear regularly and each update has new features. If you are buying, you need to start by collecting information about all that is available so that you can compare costs and capabilities. It is possible to buy videocassettes in any of these three formats, but if you intend to hire or borrow cassettes then you should check which formats will be available to you. There are some questions you should ask yourself.

(a) Player or recorder?

This is a decision that arises with videocassette machines because players are cheaper than recorders. You need a recorder if you want to do any of these things:

(i) Record 'off-air'   This is done by linking the recorder to a TV so that you can record television programmes as they are broadcast.

(ii) Copy video recordings   This is done by connecting one recorder to another recorder or to a player.

(iii) Record your own material   This is done by plugging a video camera into a recorder.

(b) Monitor or TV set?

Monitors now tend to be more expensive and restrict you to video playback only. The decision here will depend on whether or not you want to be able to watch broadcast TV.

(c) Colour or black and white?

This question is almost obsolete as far as the classroom is concerned, since almost all programmes are made in colour and you are likely to lose impact and sometimes visual information by viewing them in black and white. It is however worth remembering that black and white TV sets are now very cheap, and if, for instance, you are setting up previewing facilities for teachers a small black and white monitor or TV set is all you need.

Optional extras

(a) Remote control keypads

These are now supplied automatically with some machines. If they are not they should be bought. They make it easier for teachers to use the video machine without being tied to its side whenever they want to stop or start it.

(b) External speakers

These are well worth considering since listening is such an important activity in language learning. The sound from a TV receiver or a monitor can be improved by feeding it through an external speaker. This can be hung on a classroom wall and it can double as a speaker for audio machines.

(c) Trolleys

A trolley or cabinet with two shelves is another practical addition to the video system. This means that the player and the monitor can be kept together and moved around as one unit. Check that both shelves are the right height. The top shelf needs to be high enough for the monitor to be seen from the back of the room over rows of heads. The shelf below for the player needs to be high enough to give teachers easy access to the controls. Trolleys designed for the home don't meet these requirements.

What type of installation?

Many institutions start with one machine which is housed in the 'video room'. Teachers and classes go to the room to use the machine. Sessions may be timetabled on a regular basis - once a fortnight or once every five lessons, say - or it may be left to teachers to request the room when they want to use video.

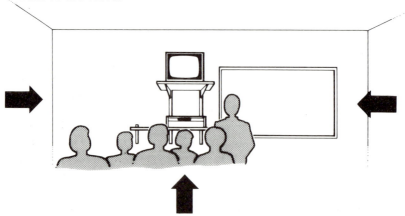

One video room shared by everyone

An alternative is to put the VCR and monitor on a trolley and make the system mobile. Teachers then book it in advance for a particular room at a particular time.

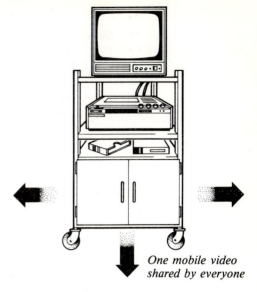

One mobile video shared by everyone

The choice between these two approaches will be governed by practical considerations such as the layout of the building. Whether the machine goes to the class or the class goes to the machine, it is a good idea to devise ways of recording how often it is used. This lets you monitor the demand that there is for it and will provide a sound basis for decisions about the possible expansion of your video facilities in the future.

One other method of distribution found in some large institutions is the 'closed circuit' system, which is really a form of broadcasting within the institution. With this system, video programmes are relayed from one central player to any number of monitors in classrooms. Programmes are booked in advance for a particular room at a particular time and are then 'broadcast' into that room as prearranged. This is a good system for some educational purposes - for example the provision of inserts to lectures - but it does not always give the user the control of the machine which makes video such an effective tool in language teaching. There are some versions of remote replay which do give the user complete remote control.

The fact that many of us start with one playback system housed in a special 'video room' encourages the analogy with the language laboratory - and we don't usually think of installing a second language laboratory unless it's a very big institute. A better analogy is with the classroom audio cassette recorder, which is a standard classroom aid in many schools and colleges nowadays. As teachers become familiar with video, and as more materials appear, it will become an aid they want to have easily to hand to use whenever it suits them. It is wise to plan for this and to keep in mind the possibility of building up to having video installed in a percentage of the classrooms. It is in any case always sound practice to start with two machines rather than one, so that there is a backup machine if one breaks down. This can double as the machine teachers use to preview materials and to find a place on a tape before a lesson. A video system can be built up gradually from there, with additions when you have proved the need for them. The table on page 8 summarises how this can be done.

HOW TO BUILD UP FROM A SINGLE VCR

MINIMUM EQUIPMENT COMBINATION	POSSIBILITIES
BASIC SYSTEM: 　　　VCR + TELEVISION RECEIVER	You can play back video or television and record off-air.
plus 　　　VCP (videocassette *player*)	You can copy from VCP onto VCR.
plus 　　　MONITOR	Linked to VCP, this gives a second playback system (this could be a small black and white monitor for teachers' use).
plus 　　　FURTHER VCPs + MONITORS	As required to expand classroom systems.
plus 　　　SECOND VCR + TV	Back-up if heavy use is made of the basic system.
ONE CAMERA	Linked to VCR, this makes your own recording possible (see Chapter 2 on recording).
plus 　　　PORTABLE VCR	Gives a mobile recording system.
plus 　　　CAMERA + VISION MIXER	Makes it possible to record onto one VCR using two cameras.
plus 　　　EDITING SUITE	Editing

Compatibility　　Compatibility is a big problem with video. Attempts to exchange materials, or to show your tapes at a conference, can very easily be thwarted if you are not aware of all the possible variations. There are different formats: VHS, Betamax, U-matic, the Philips VCR range, and not one of these is compatible with the other. A VHS machine cannot play back a Betamax cassette. There are also different colour coding systems in operation in different parts of the world. The three standards most commonly in use are PAL, SECAM, and NTSC. Some playback machines are multi-standard and can switch from PAL to SECAM or NTSC, but don't assume anything about video machines you are going to use. If you are arranging any function which involves the use of video, it is safest to specify as precisely as you can both the format and the colour system you will need or can offer.

Maintenance　　Another very important consideration is maintenance. Don't buy any video equipment without a reliable guarantee of maintenance and repair services. Find out if there is anyone in the firm you are buying from with training in the maintenance of the particular system, and the particular version of it, that you are considering. In some circumstances it is possible to arrange for training for someone from your own institution. As technology is developing so rapidly this is a factor it is very necessary to check. Otherwise there can be long delays while machines are sent away, or queue up for attention from the one person in the country who knows how they operate.

2

A guide
to video recording systems

This chapter is for those who may need to make decisions about equipping a teaching institution with video recording hardware. It will not go into technical detail but aims to provide an introduction to what is needed in terms of equipment, skills and people.

The first decision to be faced is whether the institution needs to be able to make its own recordings. 'Getting video' does not need to include getting a video camera at all. Video playback may well be all that is required. However you do need to think of getting your own camera if you want to do any of these things in your own institution:

— record student performance (Chapter 7);

— record examples of classroom practice (Chapter 9);

— record events, such as guest lectures and seminars (Chapter 9);

— collect examples of language in use in real situations (Chapter 11);

— make your own materials for the institute's teaching or teacher training programmes (Chapters 9 and 11).

These possible uses are described in detail in the chapters indicated. Here they are a reminder that you need to think about what you want to do with recording equipment before you can make sensible decisions about what you need. It is of course very difficult to predict all the uses you might make of a new technology until you have had time to experiment with it, so the same golden rule applies to recording as to playback: start small with a basic system to which you can add.

It's not just a question of deciding what you want to use a camera for; you also need to think about the quality you want. How polished do you expect the results to be? How polished do they have to be? The standards of in-house production depend on several factors:

— the range of equipment you have, particularly whether or not you have editing facilities;
— the technical quality of the equipment you have;
— the operational skills available among the staff;
— the production skills available among the staff;
— the time available.

These factors are analysed in this chapter and discussed in relation to types of production in the relevant chapters later in the book.

Hardware choices: recording

To record, you need light plus four other items: a camera, a microphone, a videorecorder and a cassette.

A camera

A microphone

A videorecorder

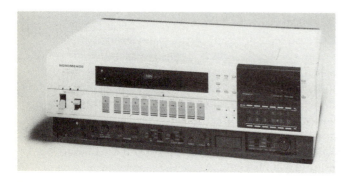

A cassette

The microphone may be built into the camera, in which case it is an omnidirectional microphone which picks up sound in a very general way.

A portable system with smaller VCR and built-in microphone

The latest development in the technology is to build in the recorder as well, making the whole thing highly portable.

A camera with the recorder built in as well

With other systems you can buy a camera which will plug into a videocassette recorder you already have. Alternatively some manufacturers produce recorders which are highly portable and have special built-in features such as an editing capability and the capacity to produce your own word captions. Most cameras now on the market are colour cameras. Those aimed at the domestic market usually have very simply operated controls and many can operate in normal lighting conditions.

So the most basic camera kit would be a camera, with its own microphone and a compatible video recorder. Possible additions to the system are:

(a) An external microphone plus stand

Usually this will cut out the internal mike when plugged in. Some recorders can take two external mikes. This is the most useful optional extra, particularly for classroom recording where sound is always a problem. Microphones are built to pick up sound from specific directions. In-built camera mikes are omnidirectional and therefore indiscriminate in the sound they pick up. In classrooms a directional mike can give you a much better chance of recording only the sound you want instead of all the sound in the room. You can also record stereo sound with some systems.

(b) Additional lights

If you will be recording in rooms with poor natural or artificial light you can get special lights to boost the light you have. Those most commonly used with domestic equipment have a power rating of 850VA and are known as 'redheads'.

Don't use extra lights unless you have to because they make small spaces very hot very quickly and they can make a classroom recording a very uncomfortable experience for everyone.

A microphone with its own stand

Additional light

Hardware choices: Editing

So far we have looked only at what you need to record the raw material. We also need to think about the end result. If you want to be at all selective about what is recorded or about what is viewed, you need to be able to edit in some way. There are several ways of editing material.

You can edit 'in the camera'. In other words you can stop and start while you are making a recording so that you make your selection on the spot. Some camera systems don't make a clean cut when you do this: the picture rolls or breaks up in some way. However this is another area where the technology is improving fast and the latest cameras have a built-in edit facility. When you use this you are editing the event as you record it so you need to have a clear plan as to what you want to record and what you don't.

You can edit by copying the sections you want onto another tape. For this you need one recorder, the 'master machine' you copy onto, and one other 'slave' machine to copy from. This can be a player (which is cheaper) or another recorder. You can assemble selections from several tapes in this way.

One problem with this kind of editing is that you may not get a clean cut at the points where you stop and start. Sometimes the picture breaks up or rolls. This is because video machines need to synchronise and not all are built to do this.

There are also more sophisticated video editing suites which consist of a master and a slave machine linked through an editing unit which synchronises the two. This offers more options and would be worth considering if you are going to do a lot of editing.

Editing can range from simple assembly of 'chunks' from different recordings, to complex production which requires both production and editing skills.

Two-camera systems The picture (below) shows how the normal two-camera system operates.

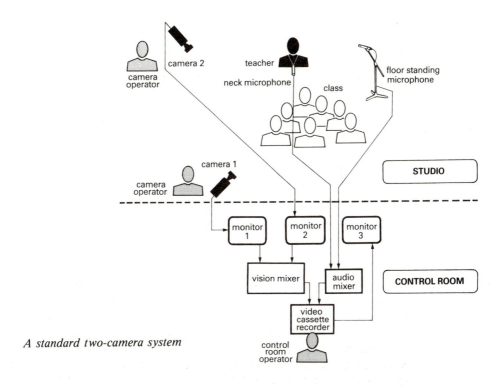

A standard two-camera system

Each camera offers a picture. The vision mixer operator selects one or the other and that picture is recorded. The operator can 'cut' from one picture to another, and is in effect editing as the recording progresses. There is continuous on-the-spot selection of the output of one camera or the other. In contrast, the output of the two microphones is combined when it is fed through the audio mixer. The operator has the choice of turning down one microphone — if for instance the class is working in groups and you only want to hear one group at a time — or of recording the combined sound of, say, teacher and student microphones on one audio track.

The whole system requires several people to operate it if it is to be used to its full capacity. It is also best to have a fixed space in which the cameras can be set up. The class has to come to the cameras rather than the camera going into the classroom. The operation of the control room equipment requires a degree of skill and understanding and therefore some specialised training is needed for anyone who is expected to use even a very simple two-camera set-up.

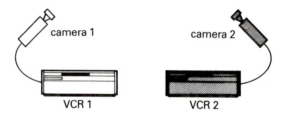

Two cameras recording separately

One other possibility is to have two cameras recording simultaneously onto two recorders. The separate recordings can then be viewed after the event and decisions about how to edit taken at that point. This is not quite as simple as it sounds: the camera operators have to shoot in such a way that their two pictures will edit together, and skilled editing is required. It is also a very time-consuming process as it of course doubles the viewing time to select what is to be edited.

Positioning one camera to record a class

Positioning two cameras to record a class (The teacher is wearing a neck microphone)

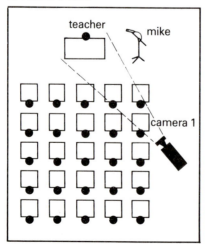

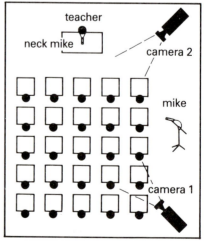

A misconception that exists about video recording of classes is that it is necessary to have a two-camera studio to do it. This is not true. Layouts can be adjusted for two-camera or single camera recording. However if you plan to do a lot of recording of teaching and can arrange for classes to come to one special recording room, you may think about a two-camera system. It is not essential for simple recording, but it does make it easier to record teacher/student interaction as it happens.

Levels of equipment

Home moviemakers are much more likely to buy a video camera than a film camera nowadays and there is a range of equipment for the domestic market which also finds its way into institutions. There are three levels of equipment, aimed at different markets and at correspondingly different price levels:

(a) Domestic
Designed for the home moviemaker, these are the cheapest systems. They record onto half-inch tape. The more expensive systems offer facilities like editing and computerised caption generation. This lets you insert your own titles and other word captions. Half-inch cassette formats: VHS, Betamax.

(b) Industrial/Commercial
An intermediate level, these are robuster machines, which record onto three-quarter-inch tape with correspondingly better quality. They also have two audio tracks. Three-quarter-inch cassette formats: U-matic Low-Band — widely used in industry and in institutions; U-matic High-Band — acceptable for broadcast, better quality than low-band, needs to be transferred to low-band to play back on that standard but will playback on low band equipment as black and white picture of variable quality.

(c) Broadcast
The best quality, recording onto ½-inch, one-inch or two-inch tape machines, used in large broadcasting stations.

Levels of skill and staffing

It is not always easy to estimate what level of skill and therefore what training will be required to make the best use of video equipment in an institution. For simple recording with no editing using a single camera system the skills needed can be acquired from reading the manual and developed by using the camera. More complex production requires skilled camera operation and skilled editing. It also requires the skills a producer deploys in planning and directing the production of separate elements which are then combined to make a finished programme.

The table below summarises the factors associated with the options we have discussed in this chapter.

SUMMARY OF RECORDING OPTIONS

single camera + mike + recorder

operation not difficult to learn
one person operation
in-camera editing
portable recorder makes location recording possible

simple editing

essential for anything beyond raw recording
useful for assembling unedited selections
requires minimal training

complex editing

requires training
requires planning
requires production skills

two-camera system

useful for classroom recording but not essential for it
requires fixed space
requires three operators
requires training
requires production skills

General advice

If you do get recording equipment, get as many people as possible familiar with how to set it up and operate it. Don't let it become the jealously guarded property of one person — treat it as one more tool for teachers to use, not as specialist equipment only the technician is allowed to touch. The more people get their hands on it, the more it is likely to be used.

Monitor the use made of it and assess recording proposals in terms of the time they will take, and the usefulness of the end result.

Keep it simple and be realistic about the production standards that can be achieved.

Institutions which do produce more complex programmes as a regular feature of their work need to have someone in charge of the operation to ensure that proper planning is done. It is best if this person can be someone who is or has been a teacher and who can therefore understand and evaluate production proposals that come up. Production planning is discussed in Chapter 11.

Arrange reliable maintenance and repair services.

3

A guide to video software

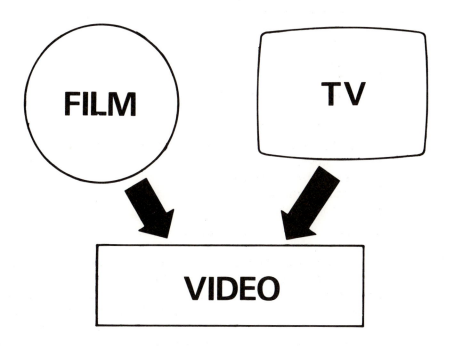

Broadcast television can be recorded off-air onto videotape. Film can also be copied onto videotape. Film and TV were with us before video came into our homes and then into our classrooms. It is not surprising therefore that the first video materials that came with video into the classroom were materials which had been made originally as films or broadcast television programmes. That means that they were designed to be viewed right through at one sitting. If they were educational programmes they probably had their own teaching built in too.

Think of the difference it makes when you can look at programmes like that in the classroom on a video player: you can stop the programme at any point, you can go back and look at something again, you can choose to break it up into as many short sections as you want to and you can come back to it another day to refresh students' memories. In other words you the teacher can do the teaching, using the video programme in whatever way you choose. This makes a big difference to the way materials should be designed and affects factors like these:

(a) Length

Broadcast schedules have to be planned in advance, programmes go out at regular times and have slots of fixed length. These slots are not usually shorter than fifteen minutes and they will often be twenty to thirty minutes long. Even a fifteen-minute programme will take up a considerable amount of lesson time if it is used at all flexibly, with pauses for discussion and repeat viewings of some sections. When you are using a set of materials in the classroom, the important thing is that it should be the right length:

    (i) for the use you want to make of it;
    (ii) for your particular students;
    (iii) for the lesson time you have.

All of these elements can vary. You can do more than just watch a programme once, straight through. Two minutes of video can provide an hour of classroom work, or it can be used to introduce a change of activity for five minutes. A ten-minute programme could be suitable for advanced learners who could follow it without difficulty. Less advanced learners would want something much shorter because their limited command of the language also limits their attention span.

(b) Continuity features

A series which is broadcast each week has a number of features designed into it to help viewers recognise 'their' programme and encourage them to watch it at the same time every week. The feeling of continuity is achieved in a variety of ways:

(i) Title music Combined with a title design, this is usually repeated at the beginning and the end of each programme and helps give it an identity.

(ii) Familiar faces The same presenter will introduce the programme each week and may appear between items to give explanations and introduce the next sequence. This person fulfils the role of teacher within the programme. Familiar faces can also be established by keeping the same characters throughout the series in the same roles.

(iii) Programme format The format of the programme is usually held constant throughout the series. This may be a magazine format which consists of different 'slots' within the programme where a particular activity is repeated each time. With educational broadcasts a fixed format has the advantage that teachers and students come to know what to expect. They know, for instance, that the English Language programme on TV will consist of Part One — a short scene, Part Two — an explanation of the language in it, Part Three — a second scene which finishes the story.

These features give continuity to broadcast programmes but this kind of continuity is not so important with classroom materials. When you can use video as another classroom aid, when and how it suits the language programme you are teaching, you almost certainly won't want to use it in the same way at the same time each week. So features like a standard format no longer have the function they have in broadcast television. A long title sequence, for example, is not necessary and can be positively irritating if you rewind too far and have to sit through it again when you want to repeat the programme. However the influence of television practice is strong and many publishers of classroom video materials for language teaching have opted for continuity of character, an ongoing story and a repeated format.

Video material designed for English language teaching

Appendix 1 gives a list of fifty-three titles of published and forthcoming ELT video materials. Something like twenty-five of these have appeared in the last two years and more are on the way. The earlier materials were almost all produced for television broadcast as well as classroom use. *Follow Me*, for example, was produced in association with several German television companies for a group of evening institutes in Germany. Its aim was to attract home viewers to evening classes to learn English. It is designed for broadcast into the home and for viewers who may be studying on their own. This is not to say that a series like *Follow Me* cannot be used in the classroom, but it is organised in a different way from materials like *Let's Watch* or *Video English* which were made specifically for classroom use. The fact that so many new titles are appearing suggests that publishers now reckon that video is getting established in language institutes. At the same time the emphasis is quite naturally shifting from production for broadcast to production for use on video in the classroom.

We can classify ELT video materials according to the role they give video in the classroom. If you look at the range now available, they suggest that we could use video for these purposes:

— presenting language;
— presenting the country and its culture;
— telling stories;
— presenting topics.

Of course most materials do several of these things at once. A series like *Family Affair*, for instance, tells a story, sets a particular cultural scene and presents specific language items in every episode. And in fact there are also topics to be drawn from the elements of the story — such as youth unemployment or divorce. But one of these four has been the starting point for the designers of the materials, and it usually therefore leads the rest. This section discusses ELT video materials under these headings as a way of relating them to the roles we can give video in the classroom. Full details of the titles mentioned can be found in Appendix 1.

Presenting language

The main aim of several sets of video materials is to present examples of language in use in an appropriate context. The first four cassettes of *Video English* contain sets of short sequences showing language functions in use in a range of situations. I have already mentioned *Family Affair*, which features specific language items selected according to the same functional and structural syllabus as the language course *Building Strategies. Let's Watch* also presents structures and functions within a story and introduces different styles of language — narrative documentary style as well as different levels of conversational style. *The English Teaching Theatre Video* is a translation to video of sketches performed by this group featuring language items.

These and other language-based materials are offered as supplementary materials which will slot into a range of syllabuses. They are intended to be used to consolidate or to revise language which has already been presented in other ways. *Follow Me*, which is also mainly a vehicle for language items, is different in that some sections are designed as the first introduction to a language item. This is a reflection of the fact that the series was designed primarily for broadcast and the producer had to cater for those home viewers who might be quite new to the language it presents.

A few series include sections where the viewing student is expected to speak. *It's Your Turn To Speak* repeats a situation with the camera taking the position of one character. The student is cued to speak the lines of this character. *Let's Watch* also has some exercises which encourage the viewer to interact with what is happening on the screen.

A set of mime sketches under the title *Speak Easy* provide a different kind of stimulus to oral production. Here no language is presented in the programme, but the situations mimed are ones where the language would be fairly predictable. In producing their own versions of what the dialogue might have been, students will be practising language they are studying in their textbooks.

Presenting the country and its culture

Video is a good way of showing students something of the country that speaks the language they're studying. Most video materials do this anyway, just by showing people with objects in a setting, particularly if it is a real setting. But some are designed specifically to feature information about the social, cultural or professional life of the country.

Focus on Britain and *Welcome to Britain* are both aimed at the young European visitor to Britain and feature domestic situations of the kind an exchange-scheme student might meet. *Challenges*, which was one of the first British series to be produced for non-broadcast use, consists of a set of six programmes, each with a different theme, and each featuring young British people engaged in pursuits typical of their age and culture. *Follow Me to San Francisco* follows the adventures of a newcomer to San Francisco and through his adventures introduces information about some aspects of that society.

Several programmes, as their titles suggest, present aspects of life in Britain: *At Home In Britain* and *Britain Now*, for example. Other titles, such as *Living in New York* and *Living in Washington* equally emphasise the cultural background they present.

Telling stories

In some cases the starting point for a set of language materials has been quite simply the power of the medium to tell a good story. This group includes detective stories, like a series based on the Sherlock Holmes stories, and adventure stories like *The Adventures of Charlie McBride* and *Brighton Pictures*. In *Video English* cassettes VC5 and VC6, each sequence tells a different story. The problem facing the characters in each one provides a narrative thread and also provides a viewing task for students. Stories on video tap the interest most of us have in the lives and predicaments of other human beings and can be used to spark off discussion in the classroom.

Several productions for children feature stories about children. These include *Here We Come, Come and See Us* and *Double Trouble* — all aimed at children between the ages of ten and fifteen. *Play and Say* uses puppets to present language and activities in a way which will interest young children.

Presenting topics

Video can bring an assortment of people into the classroom and through them a range of issues. Some materials are intended to let teachers use this facet of video as a basis for project work or to generate debate. *Video English* cassettes VC7 and VC8, for advanced level students, seek to present issues in such a way that students will make a real commitment to one point of view and will therefore engage in real debate about it. For example, there are scenes of people being interviewed for jobs of different kinds, where the viewer is left to make the final decision as to who should get the job. A forthcoming collection of BBC Archive material, *Television English*, will make available for language teaching documentary materials on a range of topics, selected primarily for the interest of the topics they present.

ESP materials

Examples on video of people at work can be very useful for students of English for a specific purpose. Several publishers have produced video recordings of meetings, for instance. *Visitron: the Language of Presentations* is a simulation of a high-level business presentation within a large company. This is used as the basis for practice in the skills of making such a presentation and of commanding the language to do it. The ESP series covering *Engineering, Business* and *Travel and Tourism* takes a different approach and records real discussions between real people working in a factory, the travel industry and an office.

Other ESP series such as *The Bellcrest Story, The Sadrina Project* and the more recent *Bid for Power* are all built around a strong storyline.

Self-study courses

As I said earlier, courses which are to be broadcast into people's homes have to cater for the individual studying alone. However this is beginning to apply to classroom video materials too as more and more people today have video machines at home. Several series are accompanied by books which aim to help the individual work alone with the video materials, and one, *Framework English* is specifically described as a self-study course. This aspect of video use is discussed in Chapter 10.

Sources of non-ELT materials

It is always a good idea to look at all possible sources of software for a new medium. This section surveys sources of non-ELT video material you might have access to.

Broadcast television	With a videocassette *recorder* (but not a video player) you can record off-air. In a country which broadcasts programmes in English this is an obvious source of material. However you will need to find out about the laws governing off-air recording in the country you are in. In Britain it is possible for an educational institution to obtain a licence to record a very limited range of programmes categorised as educational. Various schemes are being proposed to make it possible to record a wider range off-air for educational purposes but it is a complicated business involving different independent TV and production companies, different unions and a copyright law that needs to be reformed.
Video hire	Wherever sales of videocassette machines are booming, there is an accompanying boom in video hire facilities. Again you will need to investigate the legality of hiring for classroom use but where it is legal this can give you access mainly to feature films, cartoons for children and possibly to some documentary series.
Purchase	You can buy a range of materials on videocassette. TV companies market some of their TV output, for example documentary series and educational programmes, and the choice is increasing with the growing video market. There has been some production specifically for sale on video of programmes which cater for leisure interests — 'teach-yourself' golf, cookery, gardening and so on. Universities and colleges produce video materials in a range of subject areas and this is often available at low cost through special exchange schemes. See Appendix 2 for information about catalogues.
	Series which are marketed for other fields of training can sometimes be used effectively in language teaching. For example, the Video Arts materials for management skills and other training are popular with language teachers. With the advent of videodisc we can expect to see an increase in video training materials and information databases of various kinds. These will be another source if videodisc comes into the classroom.
Public information services	Both the North Americans and the British produce regular programmes in English for TV and film screening abroad. These are usually news and current affairs programmes giving information about the UK or the USA and are available free, or on subscription from the respective embassies or information services. The tone of these programmes tends to be relentlessly promotional, but the occasional clip might be useable and it's a source worth investigating if you are short of materials.
Things to look for in non-ELT materials	Programmes which were made for a general public of native speakers of the language will obviously not be graded for use with language students. Nor will they be constructed to highlight specific language items. You can however find materials which let you use video for some of the purposes suggested in the previous section.
	Perhaps the most obvious use you can make of non-ELT materials on video is to introduce topics which are relevant to your students. You may also find stories which interest and appeal. Cultural background will

inevitably be there in some way. And you might even find the occasional short sequence that features language you are studying in class. We will go on to consider possibilities offered by different types of TV and film material you might have on video. First, however, some general points to check when you are looking at non-ELT materials.

Density of language

Are there natural pauses in the flow of language which give the viewer time to let it sink in and take shape in the mind? This is particularly important for elementary students as it helps them keep pace with the programme and therefore gives them confidence in their ability to cope with longer stretches of language.

Visual support

Do the visual signals you receive help you understand the verbal messages? You can test this by turning the sound down the first time you look at the programme. How well can you guess what is happening? Can you predict the language you will hear when you turn the sound up? A close link between what the picture tells you and what the sound conveys is important for elementary level students. They need all the help they can get in following a language they don't know at all well. For more advanced students, on the other hand, you may be looking for material where the pictures give less support and the comprehension challenge is correspondingly greater.

Delivery

Do the characters speak very quickly? Do they swallow their words? Are the accents strongly regional and therefore perhaps unfamiliar to your students? Remember that the language is spoken at normal speed for an audience of native speakers. It may pose many more problems than you had anticipated. On the other hand, you may be looking for video material which gives your students the experience of listening to speech against background noise, coming from speakers who are making no concessions to their listeners.

Pause points

Look for bits of the programme that could stand on their own. Material not designed for the classroom may well be too long for a normal lesson period, so you will want to note points at which you could come in and out of the programme. The sections you choose need to make sense when viewed in isolation as well as yielding the kind of work you want to generate in the class.

You should also note points where a pause could be made for recap on the story so far or for prediction of what might happen next.

A basic plan for selecting non-ELT video

1. View the material before you teach it.
2. View it without sound first time through. (If it's too long to do this right through, view the first few minutes without sound.)
3. Note your thoughts about what you've seen. (Who are the characters? What is the setting? What is the programme about?)
4. View it again with sound.
5. If you think you might use the programme, try to list your reasons:
   What will you use it for and with which students?
   What part of your syllabus could it link in to?

Are there any other materials you could use with it?
Why will your students like it?
What do you expect them to understand from it?
6. Note ideas about how you will use it:
What techniques might work?
How much time will it need?
What preparatory work is necessary?

Types of non-ELT material

If you have access to any of the sources I have mentioned, you will have a choice of several different types of 'text'. Just as you might make a selection of examples of written English from newspapers, journals, academic textbooks or works of fiction, so you can have video material of very different styles and construction. This section looks at those you are most likely to have access to and suggests ways of assessing their suitability as an aid to language learning. Ways of using them are discussed in the next three chapters.

Drama

Under this heading come feature films, broadcast plays, 'soap opera' serial stories, 'sitcom' comedy series. Common to them all is the fact that they are acted and are therefore simulations of reality, which may be done with varying degrees of realism or fantasy. Their value for a language learner is that they contain all kinds of examples of people communicating.
Things to look for in selecting dramatic material are:

(a) Segments that can stand on their own
Assuming you are going to want to use the material as a normal part of a normal lesson, when you look at a drama you will be looking for short segments which can stand on their own sufficiently to make sense as an independent sequence. Examples of the kind of short scene you might pick out of a drama are:

— a new arrival joins a group, is introduced, conversation resumes;

— a customer comes into a shop, asks for something, buys it and leaves;

— an argument starts, reaches a climax, is resolved;
— a problem arises, solutions are suggested, one is tried and succeeds or fails.

(b) Content

You would, of course, not be likely to select a sequence just because it would stand on its own. You will also be looking for content you could exploit in the language classroom. Some popular TV series can be rich in examples of language functions in use, for instance, because they feature domestic situations such as shopping, entertaining, meeting new people and so on. Sometimes you might be looking for examples of certain kinds of behaviour — how do you go about persuading people to do things in certain situations? What do you do when you need information and nobody is being helpful? How does the behaviour of different people compare when each is faced with the same problem? At other times you may simply be looking for a good story with situations and characters which will interest and entertain your students.

(c) A warning about selecting drama excerpts

It is easy to describe the kinds of sequence you could hope to find in dramatic material. Indeed as you watch drama on television you often think 'That's just what I want for tomorrow's lesson.' However when you come to pin it down, you find that it is not all that easy to find bits which feature exactly what you want in the way and at the length you want them. Often a lot of necessary information about characters or plot has been established in previous episodes or the language items you're interested in are lost in a flow of language your students couldn't cope with. It can take a lot of viewing time to build up a library of useable sequences.

Documentary

Documentary programmes present topics. They give factual information and opinions about aspects of the world and they are likely to contain some of these elements:

(a) A commentary

This links all the other elements. It is often spoken by a presenter who may never appear on the screen but is heard partly or entirely as 'voice over'. Commentary of this kind is usually very carefully and skilfully scripted to match the pictures it accompanies.

(b) Location inserts

These are sequences which have been filmed outside the studio. The camera takes the audience into the situation, brings home the reality of a problem, makes vivid the emotions of the participants. Location inserts potentially give the strongest visual clues to programme content. However they can be used just as 'wallpaper' to fill the screen while the words carry the message. In this case they may not add anything at all to the message.

(c) People talking

Documentaries often include interviews with people who have some connection with the topic. The interviewer's questions may be edited out so that all we see is the individual talking although the interviewer was in fact standing slightly to the left or right of the camera.

Sometimes part or all of a commentary is given by people who are featured in the programme. This kind of commentary is usually produced by means of an interview, although again the interviewer's questions will often be edited out so that the commentary sounds like continuous speech. This kind of commentary is not scripted. So this element in documentary programmes is a good source of examples of authentic, spontaneous speech.

Things to look for in selecting documentary material are:

(i) Content

You are most likely to select documentary material for its subject matter. The most important question is therefore: Is the topic of interest to your students? Is it something they want to know about? Can it be related in any way to their own experience? For example is there something similar happening in their own country so that they might compare and contrast practice in one country and another?

Another question to consider is whether you have any other materials dealing with the same topic. If you have you could perhaps use them along with the video text as a package grouped around a theme.

(ii) Visual support

A lot of the visual support in drama comes from the gestures and facial expressions of the actors. The visual element of documentary material is quite different — at least when location shots are used. In this case some visuals match the verbal commentary very closely and others tell their own complementary story, adding to the information the words convey. Some positively conflict by setting off a train of thought which is quite at variance with the message the audio track carries. Our eyes take in more information than any other of our senses. The visual channel is capable of being a powerful distractor instead of an essential part of the message. Think about this when you preview documentary material and be aware of the effect the visual element may have on your students when they view. Is it likely to be a help or a hindrance?

(iii) A warning about selecting documentary material

The danger with documentary material is that, because much of the information tends to be carried verbally, we begin to concentrate on that and to ignore the visual. Try to select material which uses pictures to tell at least some of the story and then make sure that you exploit this in your use of it in the language class.

Current affairs and
news programmes

News and current affairs programmes are the television equivalent of newspapers. They are similar to documentary programmes except that the content is more ephemeral as, by definition, the programmes have to be topical. They have their own formats. One or sometimes two newsreaders or reporters present straight to the camera, and these 'talking heads' often have some form of visual 'headline' behind them. This is a box with words or a picture which changes when the reporter moves to a new topic. The programmes also contain location footage of varying lengths.

Things to look for in current affairs material are:

(a) Content

The interest and relevance of the topic will probably be your prime concern in selecting material of this kind. It is in the nature of this kind of programme that it deals with several different topics, so the length of individual items is likely to be good for classroom use. A lot of current affairs material has a very short life and if you are receiving programmes from another country you will also have the problem of sifting out items which assume detailed knowledge of local events and personalities because they won't mean much to your students. You could draw up a checklist of topics which are of current concern to your students to help you select suitable items from news programmes.

(b) Visual support

This kind of programme will have a higher proportion of 'talking heads' than any of the other types discussed here. This doesn't mean that there are no visual clues to understanding: we all unconsciously use lip and head movements to help us make out what a speaker is saying. However this may not give a learner as much help as they can get from seeing the actions, people, objects and settings location footage will contain. Look for programmes that have a high proportion of such visual support.

(c) A warning about selecting current affairs material

Teachers often say they want this kind of material because of its interest value. Remember however that current affairs and news programmes are rooted in the moment and the particular local concerns of the country that produces them. You will need a steady supply of up-to-date programmes if you are to exploit their topical nature and you will need to be able to preview regularly to select what is appropriate. It would be a good idea to develop a formula for using this kind of programme so that you know precisely what kind of item you are looking for and, if you *can* arrange for a regular supply, you don't need to spend a lot of time viewing it to work out how you are going to use it.

Cartoons

There is a large selection of animated cartoons produced for children. They are usually short, they have a clear storyline, they are humorous. They place at least one of their characters in a string of predicaments to which there are fantastic solutions. The characters are often familiar ones and their predicaments although far-fetched can be predicted by anyone who makes a habit of watching cartoons.

Apart from cartoons aimed at entertaining children, they are also used in educational programmes for children and sometimes for adults and they frequently feature in advertisements.

Things to look for when selecting cartoons are:

(a) Characters

Are they familiar ones? Can your students tell you stories about them? Do they also feature in cartoons in print which you might use along with the video programme? Are they the kind of characters your students will identify with and therefore want to discuss?

(b) Visual support

Visuals are a strong element in cartoons. How clearly do they tell the story? Even if the language is hard to follow could your students retell the story from watching the visuals only? What happens if you run fast forward in vision? Can you still make out the storyline? (This could be a way of 'skim viewing' a longer cartoon story.)

(c) Sound effects

Music and sound effects are usually an important part of a cartoon. Do they help you to follow the story? Could you exploit this by starting with the soundtrack without the picture? (This technique is described in Chapter 4.)

(d) A warning about selecting cartoons

Pay particular attention to the language used in cartoons. It may be very colloquial and the voices are often distorted. Does this make them difficult to follow? Will your students be able to cope with this?

While the visuals usually tell the story, remember that we lose the support of many of the visual elements we get in realistic presentations — lip movements for example.

Advertisements

If you can get hold of examples, some TV advertisements are excellent aids for language teaching: they are short and very carefully planned; every word and every visual is there by design and for specific effect. They can contain good examples of language put to a very precise use, and are particularly likely to yield examples of some kinds of language — the language of description and the language of persuasion are two obvious examples. They are also of interest from a different point of view. Some students would be interested in the way the medium is used to convey a message. You could use them to study the language and techniques of advertising.

A warning about selecting advertisements Many advertisements play with the meanings of words. This may be clever and amusing, but you will have to decide whether it would make them too obscure for your students. If it takes a lot of explanation from you before they can see the point, is it a worthwhile exercise? You would need to be selective and have many to choose from if you wanted to make regular use of this kind of material.

Authenticity

A claim made for non-ELT television materials is that they are authentic. This is a word which is used with different meanings in different contexts. When it is applied to video materials for language teaching, it mostly seems to mean that the materials were made for an audience of native speakers. This is in contrast to ELT materials which, in various ways, take account of the needs of learners of the language.

In other contexts 'authenticity' means natural, spontaneous use of the language but this is in practice a difficult line to draw with video materials. There are many examples of video materials produced for language learning use which nevertheless contain authentic features such as spontaneous, unscripted speech, whereas, as I pointed out in describing the content of documentaries, most commentary is carefully scripted and not therefore spontaneous.

What is perhaps more important for the language learner is that viewing television or film made for a native speaking audience is an authentic experience. It puts the learner in the same position as that audience and demands the same exercise of language skills.

This is a rewarding experience, provided that it is a successful one — which brings us to Part Two and methods of using both ELT and non-ELT materials in the classroom.

PART 2
TEACHING WITH VIDEO

4

Making the most of what it offers

What the machine can do

When it first came into the classroom video was seen as a substitute film projector or TV set. It is certainly true that it can be used in this way but it is far from being the only way to use video in the classroom — particularly in language teaching.

One useful starting point for thinking about any new piece of technology is the physical properties of the machine. What can it do and therefore what can you do with it? Here are some of the answers with video machines:

(a) Play, stop, rewind, replay

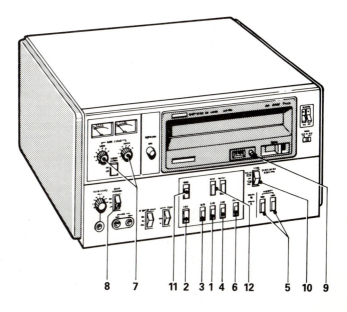

1 Play
2 Stop
3 Rewind
4 Fast Forward
5 Visual Search
6 Pause (Freeze Frame)
7 Volume (Control)
8 Channel 1
  Channel 2
9 Zero Counter
10 Programmed Operation
11 Cassette Eject
12 Record

At any point in a video recording you can stop, think about what you have seen, rewind and look at it again if you want to. This immediately makes viewing video a very different experience from viewing projected film or broadcast TV. We already exploit this facility when we use audiotape in the classroom. It is surprising how often we forget that we can do the same with video.

(b) Fast forward, rewind

There is no need to start at the beginning of a programme. You can run forward to any point you choose and simply look at one short section in the middle. Then you have the option of rewinding to look at what came before.

(c) Visual search

Not all video machines have this property but it is becoming more and more common to be able to see the picture as you run forward or back on the tape or disc. This is often called visual search or simply search, to distinguish it from fast forward, when you don't see the picture. The search facility has the practical value of making it quicker and simpler to find your place in the recording. When the picture is sharp enough on fast search (machines vary), then you have a way of skipping through a long programme, perhaps selecting only some sections for normal viewing. With the right kind of visual material you could do what we might call 'skim viewing' of the bits you don't want to spend time on.

(d) Stop, pause, freeze frame

You can stop all machines. Some of them take a second or two to stop whirring and clacking as they wind tape off a drum. Others can make a loud noise when stopped and you have to turn the volume down. Many now have a pause button which allows you to avoid these irritations and means that play starts again immediately you release pause.

Some machines have the capacity to freeze the picture on the screen when you pause and we discussed in Chapter 1 the way picture quality can vary between videodisc and videocassette when you do this.

If you do get a good still picture when you put the machine in pause, you can use this facility in the same way that you use other still pictures in the classroom. You may want to look more closely at an image which is unfamiliar. You may want to check whether your students have the vocabulary they need to talk about the programme. Even if you cannot freeze frame, the pause facility is one to exploit. I discuss later in this chapter ways of using pauses for students to repeat, answer questions or use a worksheet.

(e) Volume control

It is possible with all monitors or TV sets to turn the volume to zero. This offers us the possibility of separating the picture from the sound and the potential of this in a language classroom is great. It means that at some point in a viewing activity the learner can be asked to focus on the visual channel only. This technique of working with the sound turned off is known as silent viewing — see Video Plan 3 in this chapter.

(f) Two audio channels

Some video machines can play back two audio tracks. You can select track one or track two, or you can play a 'mix' of the two. This makes it possible, for example, to have programmes with soundtracks in two languages or to have two alternative commentaries to the same set of pictures.

If you use a videocassette recorder with this facility, check it to see if it has a socket you can plug a microphone into. If it has, you could record your own soundtrack onto one audio track on the videotape, while the recorded track remains untouched on the other. That lets you or your students put your own version of a commentary to a programme.

(g) Zero counter

Most tape and cassette machines have a zero counter. You can use it to help you find your way around a tape, rather like you use page numbers in a book. You run the tape and note the counter number at any point you wish to mark. It is useful to establish within an institute that everyone will zero at the same point, so that the numbering starts from approximately the same place each time. With videocassette machines you can do this by putting the machine into rewind mode when you first put the cassette in. Then zero the counter when the rewind process is completed.

(h) Programme memory

Some videocassette machines have a switch marked 'programmed operation' or 'programme memory'. You can set this so that the machine will stop at points you have preselected: if you zero at your starting point on the tape, the machine will stop there automatically when you rewind. You can also zero the counter at your end point on the tape, then rewind to the start point: when it plays up to 000 the machine stops the tape and rewinds to the beginning. This could be useful where a video programme was being shown continuously, as part of a display for instance.

(i) Remote control

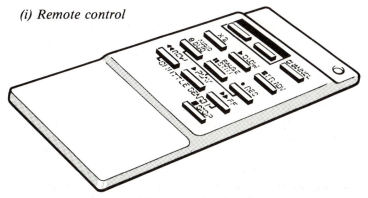

One of the most useful accessories for classroom use is a remote control unit. It may be cordless or attached by a cable to the VCR. Remote control releases you from the need to stay close to the video machine in order to operate the controls. This makes it easier to stop and start the video exactly when you want to.

**Getting to grips
with the machine**

The most important thing to remember about using video is

YOU CONTROL THE MACHINE.
THE MACHINE DOESN'T CONTROL YOU.

Many of the suggestions in this book about ways of using video assume that the person using it is familiar with what the machine can do and so feels confident about finding a place on a tape, stopping and starting at will, turning the sound up and down and so on.

Some people are very wary of machines: 'I only have to look at it and it breaks down.' This apprehension is understandable. Video machines are complex bits of technology and most of us don't begin to understand how their electronic innards work. And they do go wrong sometimes — you switch on and nothing happens, or the picture starts breaking up, or you can't get any sound. We've all had the unnerving experience of something going wrong when thirty people are sitting waiting for us to start. These things happen to the most confident of video users and the gremlins always seem to choose their moment with great care. What can you do about it?

The first thing you need to do with any machine, if you possibly can, is to give yourself a 'hands on' session to get to know how it works. Practise using it until you feel quite at home with all the knobs and buttons. This is the best way to build up your confidence. Even if you have a technician on call to deal with equipment it is a very good idea to teach yourself how to set up, plug in and check the obvious things when something goes wrong. You should aim to be using video in the classroom as easily as you use the audiocassette recorder or the Overhead Projector. If you are just starting with video, or even if you think you're very familiar with it, try running through some of these familiarisation routines:

Routine one: Basic playback routine
— Plug in to the mains (you may need to plug in player and monitor separately);
— switch on;
— put the cassette into the player;
— rewind to check that it's at the beginning of the tape;
— set the zero counter to 000;
— play the tape.
  While it's playing, experiment with the controls on the monitor to make sure you know what each one does. Then go to different parts of the room to check whether you can see and hear clearly everywhere. Note any parts of the room which are bad for viewing - you might need to move people when you're going to switch on.
— stop and rewind;
— remove the cassette;
— unplug from the mains.

Routine two: Finding your place

— Plug in ... zero the counter numbers (the same first five steps as in Routine one);
— run fast forward to 050;
— mark this as your starting point by resetting the counter to 000;
— play and check colour, volume, position of monitor;
— stop and rewind to the starting point you marked (i.e. by rewinding to 000);
— play that section without sound then rewind to replay it with sound;
— rewind to the beginning of the tape.

Note about using the zero counter:

I have already pointed out that if your machine has a programme memory you can set it to stop automatically when it reaches 000. Even if you don't have a programme memory you can use 000 to mark your place at the beginning of any section you want to replay. This makes it easy to find that point again. Sometimes you want to use several sections on one tape, playing each one more than once. You may have noted the counter numbers for each section, counting from the beginning of the tape. If you want to use the counter to mark the beginning of a section in the middle of the tape (as for section 2 in the picture below), remember this will affect the numbering for the rest of the tape.

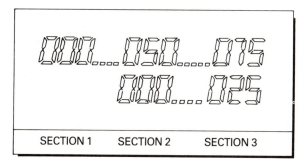

| SECTION 1 | SECTION 2 | SECTION 3 |

Routine three: Checking for faults

— Examine all the connecting cables the machine has;

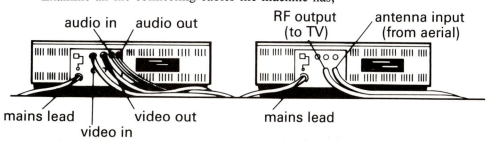

Connection between machine and TV may be by separate audio and video cables or a combined lead plugging into the TV set aerial socket

— disconnect all the cables, mix them up then try to reconnect them;
— check your machine for any controls that have more than one setting

(e.g. the TV set may have a control for selecting TV or video, the switch on U-matic players selects audio channels 1,2 or mix);

— try changing these settings to see what effect it has.

These are things to check when you have problems getting your machine to work. It's a good idea to get someone to 'throw' a few switches when you're not looking. Then test yourself on how much you've learned about the way your particular machine works. The more familiar you are with it, the more confident you will be about using it. Then you can concentrate on using it to good effect.

Techniques

Your familiarity with the machine and what it can do will suggest to you ways you can use it in your teaching. This section looks at the range of techniques you can choose from before we move on in the next chapter to examine different ways video can be related to the rest of the language programme.

Viewing the whole programme

The first option you have is to use the video just like a TV set and show a programme straight through from beginning to end. It may be difficult for you to do any more than this if your time with the video machine is very limited, and the only materials you have are non-ELT programmes. Suppose, for example, you have a thirty-minute session in the video room, once a month, and you are expected to show a twenty-minute documentary during that time. Is it worth doing? Well, in some countries this might be the only opportunity learners get to hear extensive chunks of the language, so you could treat it as a 'language bath' session and concentrate on helping your learners come away with a general idea of the content. Video Plan 1 shows how you could plan the lesson in three stages.

VIDEO PLAN 1: Viewing straight through

Stage One: Before viewing

Introduce the topic and key vocabulary.
Set one or two very general questions designed to elicit the main content points in the programme.
Try to include at least one question which focusses on information that is presented visually, so that everyone has a chance of producing an answer.

Stage Two: Play the programme

Note that it is not a good idea to ask students to make notes or complete a worksheet while they view, as this means their heads will be down and they'll miss some of the visual information.

Stage Three: Follow-up

Depending on the time you have, your discussion of the programme could continue in the classroom, but it is often difficult to revive interest if this has to wait until the next lesson. It's probably best to keep your round-up within the time available immediately after the class has seen the programme. Alternatively you could set a post-viewing writing task for homework.

Breaking it up into sections

An obvious benefit of having the video machine under your control is that you can break a programme up into sections and guide your learners through it one section at a time.

> ### VIDEO PLAN 2: Viewing in sections
>
> 1. Set previewing questions for Section One.
> 2. Play Section One.
> 3. Discuss answers for Section One questions.
>   Set previewing questions for Section Two.
> 4. Play Section Two.
> 5. Discuss answers for Section Two questions.
>   Set previewing questions for Section Three.
>
> And so on to final stage: repeat the whole programme without pauses.

You can of course treat different sections in different ways, using a variety of techniques. If you do work through a programme in sections, try to finish by playing the whole programme through without a pause, if it is not too long. This can be seen as the target activity learners are working towards during the 'viewing in sections' stage — the final extended viewing which consolidates the comprehension work that has gone before.

Select one section only

Within a long programme you may find a short sequence which contains exactly what you want for a particular lesson. If it works for your purpose there is nothing wrong with using only that sequence. Some people worry that learners will object if they don't see the whole programme. They argue that it is unnatural to break up a programme which was made to be viewed as a whole. Those who put forward this argument are thinking of video as a substitute television set. When you switch to thinking of it as just another resource in the classroom, you put it in a different perspective. Then the test of any technique you use with video becomes the same as the test of anything else you do — does it help the achievement of your objectives? The control you have over the video 'text' gives you the flexibility to use it in the way that best suits your particular purpose at any particular time.

Viewing tasks

You can see from the video plans we've already looked at that the main difference between viewing televison at home and using video in the classroom comes from the tasks you set your learners. We look and listen with more attention if we are viewing for a purpose. This also helps us remember better afterwards what we have seen and heard. That is why it's good to think about ways you can encourage your students to view actively. You can do this in different ways.

(a) Previewing questions

Before you switch on, set questions to focus students on whatever you want to highlight at that stage. At different stages in your treatment of a sequence, these questions might be about:

for drama: (i) the characters (Who are the people?), the setting (Where are they?), their roles (Why are they there? What is their relationship?), the situation (Why are they there?), the plot (What is happening?) or the language (What are they saying?).

for documentary: (ii) the topic (What is the programme about?), the setting (Where is it?), the point of view expressed (What effect does the programme seek to make?), or the language (How is ... described?).

(b) Worksheets

Another way of setting viewing tasks is to have some form of worksheet for the student to fill in during or after viewing. As we have already pointed out, it is best to build in pause points for any writing that has to be done, otherwise parts of the programme will be missed as students look down at their papers. Below are extracts from two different kinds of worksheet produced by Thames Television International for English courses.

Worksheet 1

Watch the breakfast scene WITHOUT THE SOUNDTRACK and answer the following questions.

13.   What is the atmosphere like?

14.   Describe what the different persons are doing.

AMANDA
KATHERINE
MICHAEL
JUNE
FRANK

Then watch it WITH THE SOUNDTRACK and answer the following questions.

15.   What is Frank telling Amanda?

16.   Who is on Amanda's side?

17.   Why does Katherine suddenly leave the table?

18.   Have you ever experienced a similar situation? If yes, tell me about it.

Watch the conversation between Katherine and June and tell me in your own words what the conversation was about.

(Only part of the unit is reproduced here)

Worksheet 2 | IF I RULED THE WORLD

1 Listen to this episode again - or watch it.
Take notes and make a list of things the children would do if they ruled the world; then write down the reasons you think they have for wishing these things.

	What they would do	Why do you think they'd do it?
1.		
2.		
3.		
4.		

What would you do?	Why?

2 Listen carefully to the next episode - or watch it.
The children are talking about race, colour and prejudice.

What do they they think about it?

Do you agree?

If not - what do you think about this problem?

One of the girls says:

"People judge you by the colour of your skin, and the clothes you wear, but you can't tell a book by its cover."

Translate it into your own language - then try to explain (in your own language or English) what she means by saying so. Tell me if you agree or disagree - and why.

(Only part of the unit is reproduced here)

Silent viewing

Think of all the information your eyes collect for you as you walk in the street, talk to someone, catch a train, read a newspaper, take part in a meeting. We use this information to help us interpret our surroundings and the events we observe or participate in. Visual information helps us interpret the audio signals we receive by reinforcing them with additional clues: a beckoning finger reinforces the words 'Come here'; at the same time the expression on the face of the beckoner can give us a clue as to the nature of the summons.

When learners watch video programmes in the target language, they are exercising their listening skills as they do when they listen to an audiotape. With video they have all the additional clues the visuals give them while they watch and listen. This intake of information from several sources at once is a complex process, and the value to learners of silent viewing is that it lets them concentrate on one element at a time. The first viewing of a sequence can be done without sound so that the learner has time to think about the place, the people and the situation before having to cope with what they are saying. When we talk to each other we usually take in this kind of visual information subconsciously. We are not really aware of how we draw on visual clues in our interpretation of what we hear. An initial silent viewing lets learners do consciously what we normally do subconsciously. It focusses them on some of the visual clues they might otherwise miss. It gives them time to think about this information before they tackle the listening task. In this way silent viewing is an aid to listening comprehension and the goal of comprehension is approached in two stages.

Silent viewing also generates a genuine desire to communicate within the group. We all seek to interpret what we see. We form hypotheses about the people we see on the screen — who they are, why they're there, what's going on. Even if your students have very little command of the spoken language, they will have their own ideas about what they have seen. Often there are disagreements and the desire to defend their own interpretation can lead learners to stretch their powers of communicating to the utmost.

Leading on from this, the next stage involves highly focussed listening. When viewers have had time to develop their own theories about the scene, they are strongly motivated when it comes to listening to the soundtrack to check whether or not they were right. And when they are listening in this way to check their theories they have a real purpose in listening. This can help them overcome their tendency to listen for the words rather than the message. This is an important goal in learning to communicate in a foreign language.

You can also use silent viewing to get your students practising the language. They could, for instance, roleplay the situation they have seen before they hear it with sound. This uses the picture on the screen as a stimulus to oral production and helps you check the language your learners already have at their command. So silent viewing has a diagnostic function too.

Video Plan 3 shows how you could organise silent viewing of a short sequence of about one minute.

VIDEO PLAN 3: Silent viewing

Stage One: Prepare for silent viewing

Tell the class they will see the sequence without sound and ask them to think about specific questions while they view. The questions could be:

(i) for a dialogue:
   Who are the people you see?
   Where are they?
   Why are they there?
   What are they doing?

(ii) for documentary material:
   Where is this place?
   What objects are shown?
   What is the programme about?
   What can you work out about what you see?

These first questions deliberately focus students on the situation and not the language.

Stage Two: First silent viewing

Play the sequence without sound.

Stage Three: Discussion

Class works in groups, comparing notes on their answers, followed by general round-up on group views.

AT THIS POINT YOU HAVE A CHOICE ...

Stage Four A: Second silent viewing to focus on language

This time your preview question will be: 'What are they saying?' After viewing, the group task is to predict the language they will hear. They could be asked to roleplay a dialogue or to write a commentary, depending what kind of sequence it is.

OR GO STRAIGHT ON TO ...

Stage Four B: View with sound

Play the sequence with sound. Students check their predictions about the situation, content or language, depending on the preview task they have had.

Starting with sound only

The opposite of turning down the sound is blacking out the picture. You can't usually 'turn off' the picture in the same way you can turn down the sound but there are various ways you can organise things so that the class is presented with the soundtrack only:

— You may have a copy of the soundtrack on an audio cassette.
— You can cover the screen with a piece of thick card or cloth.
— You can ask your students to turn their backs to the screen or close their eyes.
— You can turn the monitor round with its back to the class (only if you have an external speaker, otherwise the speaker in the set will be pointing away from the class and the sound will be muffled.)

What is the point of starting with audio only? After what we've said about visual support, it might seem perverse to use a video machine without

---

VIDEO PLAN 4: Starting with sound only (Using a cartoon)

Choose a section without dialogue, preferaby with a mixture of music and sound effects. Look out for places where the music is linked to a particular character, indicates a chase and so on.

Stage One: Preparation

1A. If the cartoon features well-known characters show students pictures of the main characters in the cartoon. Discuss what they know about them, what personalities they have, what kind of adventures they have, what usually happens when they meet etc.

1B. If your students won't recognise the characters, establish the names, show pictures of them if you have them, discuss in general terms what happens in the kind of cartoon you're going to show.

2. Arrange students and set so that they cannot see the screen and tell them they are going to use their imaginations to guess what is on the screen. Include questions related to the sounds they'll hear. For example:

Which character appears first?
What are they doing?
What noises can you hear? (Ask this if there are strong sound effects for things like water, sawing wood etc.)
What do you think the characters look like? (If they haven't seen pictures of them.)

Stage Two: Play the section — sound only

Stage Three: Discuss

Discuss in groups, comparing notes on answers. Try to tell the story and to predict what they will see on the screen.

Stage Four: Replay the section — picture and sound
Class looks at the section to check what really happened.

Stage Five: Preparation for continued viewing
Set preview questions for continuation of viewing, using whatever technique you choose. You could do some silent viewing with the next section, to compare the information your students can get from that.

the picture. And certainly it isn't a technique you would be likely to use frequently. However, with some materials and for some purposes it could be worth considering.

Possible reasons for starting with sound only are:

— To intrigue students and stimulate discussion among them as to what they think they will see on the screen.

— To focus on the differences between the kinds of information carried verbally and visually.

— To generate the language of description by setting students the task of describing a character or a place they are going to see.

Materials with interesting sound effects would lend themselves to this kind of treatment. Video Plan 4 on page 42 shows how you could use this technique with a cartoon.

Jigsaw viewing

If you are familiar with the term 'jigsaw listening' you will know that this involves groups of students listening to different versions of a story on audio. The story is constructed in such a way that each group gets different information, or perhaps a different version of the same story. An information gap is created and in order to tell the complete story, groups need to share the information they have. In this way they piece together all the facts.

Since video offers the possibility of separating sound from picture, and each of these channels carries its own information, it should be a good medium for this technique — jigsaw viewing instead of jigsaw listening. And it should be possible to apply it to any available material, without the need of programmes specially constructed for the purpose. What you need to work out is how to use the space and the machinery you have so that you can organise the jigsaw part with the least fuss and inconvenience.

These are some suggestions:

(a) Sound/picture split
If you have access to two rooms and an audio copy of the soundtrack, you can follow Video Plan 5A. Otherwise you could try the ideas suggested in Video Plans 5B and 5C.

VIDEO PLAN 5A: Sound/Picture split

Before the lesson

Prepare a set of questions so that some can only be answered from hearing the sound, while others relate to what is on the screen. Some examples of the kinds of questions you could ask for drama are:

ABOUT VERBAL INFORMATION	ABOUT VISUAL INFORMATION	ABOUT INFORMATION THAT MIGHT BE CARRIED EITHER WAY
What are the names of the characters?	What do they look like?	How many people are there?
What does A say to B?	How are they feeling?	Do they know each other?
What are they discussing?	What ages are they?	Where are they?
		Why are they there?
		What are they doing?

Questions you could pose for documentary are:
What is the programme about?
Describe ... (an object or a place that features in the programme; something about which there is both visual and verbal information.)

Stage One

Put the class in pairs, A and B. All the As will go into one room to listen to the sound only. All the Bs will be in the room with the video and they will see the picture without sound. Before they split up, give them all the same set of questions.

Stage Two

The two groups listen or view separately, then discuss their answers to the questions.

Stage Three

The two groups come together and pair off As and Bs. Each pair goes through their answers together, comparing notes.

Stage Four

General round-up comparing what they got from the picture with what they got from the sound. This is a point at which different interpretations might emerge.

Stage Five

Play the scene for everyone to see and hear.

(b) Picture plus sound/sound only

VIDEO PLAN 5B: Picture + Sound/Sound only

Before the lesson

Prepare the same kinds of questions as in Video Plan 5A.

Stage One

Put the class in pairs, A and B. A sits with his/her back to the screen, B sits facing it. So A can only hear the soundtrack while B sees and hears. Give them the questions.

Stage Two

Play the sequence.

Stage Three

The pairs compare notes on their answers.

Stage Four

Similar discussion to Video Plan 5A.

Stage Five

Play the whole scene through again for everyone to see and hear.

(c) Picture only/ no information

VIDEO PLAN 5C: Picture only/Nothing

Before the lesson

Place the screen, or arrange the class, so that one half can see it and the other can't.

Stage One

Turn the sound down. One half silent views, the other does nothing. (This would obviously only be suitable with a very short section of not more than about one minute.)

Stage Two

After they've seen it, the viewers report to their partners what they think was going on.

Stage Three

The whole class views with sound to see whether the viewing partners were right or not.

This often works well with the last section of a story when it's the kind of story that could have a variety of endings.

The table below summarises the techniques we have derived from an analysis of the properties of the machine.

VIDEO PLAYBACK: PROPERTIES AND TECHNIQUES	
PROPERTIES	TECHNIQUES
1 *Play/stop/rewind/fast forward/pause* Zero counter/programme memory. Remote control.	*Control by teacher in classroom* View whole programme. View in sections. Repeat whole/replay in sections. Omit sections.
2 *Sound and vision controlled separately* The volume can be turned down (but note that with most monitors you can't do the reverse and lose the picture).	*View without sound* Silent viewing of whole sequence as preparation for listening. Turn sound down at certain points for students to supply possible dialogue.
3 *Freeze frame* Pause 'freezes' picture on screen. (Not all monitors.)	*Pause + visual cue* Oral practice with 'frozen' picture as prompt. Worksheet entry. Note-taking.
4 *Two audio channels* Original soundtrack usually recorded on channel 2	*Record own commentary* Teachers record simpler version. Students record own versions.

Problems

When any new resource comes into a school two groups always seem to emerge. There's a small band of enthusiasts who devote an enormous amount of time and energy to experimenting with it and who sometimes tend to hail it as the solution to every problem. And then there are those who regard it with suspicion and distaste, forecasting all kinds of problems and very few results. This book is obviously on the side of the enthusiasts and is written in the belief that video is a definite asset in the language classroom. But it is certainly not the ultimate resource which will do the whole job for us; no classroom aid is. And it does have its attendant problems which it is only sensible to recognise. What are they and how can we deal with them?

Machine phobia

I've already referred to this syndrome. Some people are very mistrustful of machines, perhaps because they have had bad experiences with them and are therefore nervous about using them. Two things can help teachers to overcome such fears:

(a) Reliable maintenance and emergency servicing

The importance of organising a maintenance and repairs service has already been mentioned in Chapter 1. The knowledge that there is someone on call if the machine isn't working is very reassuring. But of course it is only reassuring if the person can be relied on to be there whenever the need arises — and you can be sure that that is bound to be during the last class hour on the longest teaching day of the week. Even where there is a trained video technician on the staff it's a good idea to train others to check for basic faults. Arrange things so that there is always someone in the building who is on call for machine problems. It's also a good idea to have a spare machine readily to hand and regularly checked so that it can be wheeled in at a moment's notice.

(b) Orientation sessions for all users

Familiarity with machines breeds confidence in using them. All teachers should be given time to get to know the machines they are expected to use as well as the materials they will use with them. The section on 'Getting to grips with the machine' earlier in this chapter includes some suggestions for familiarisation routines to introduce teachers to their video equipment.

Passive viewing

Most of us, at least occasionally, go home, switch on the TV, switch off our minds, stretch out in a comfortable chair and let the box keep us entertained for the evening. We bring these habits to video too — especially when it is treated as a substitute TV. The guiding principle is that our minds are more active when we view with a purpose. And we have that purpose if we know in advance that we are looking for the answers to certain questions, or that we will be asked to carry out certain tasks as a result of viewing. The techniques discussed earlier in this chapter all contribute to making viewing an activity with a purpose. It's worth pointing this out to your students too, so that they understand why you set the tasks you do when you use video with them.

Preparation time

You will not use a video sequence effectively in the classroom unless you have looked at it beforehand. Reading the script is not sufficient. You may miss all kinds of things you could exploit. In fact you probably need to view several times to check possibilities and to decide how you will treat the material. The problem of course is getting access to a machine and finding time to do all the viewing you want. It is suggested in Chapter 1 that, even where there is only one video room, it is wise to have a fallback video player in case of breakdown. If this can be kept in a place that is accessible to teachers, along with a monitor (a small black and white one would do), then it can be used for teacher viewing and for setting a tape at the right place before a lesson.

Limited software

The problem with new technology is that the hardware is always ahead of the software. And without the right materials it is difficult to exploit the resource to the full. The techniques we have looked at are more effective with some types of material than others and we want materials that can take a sensible place in our scheme of work. Fortunately the situation is beginning to improve and, as we have seen, more video material is now being published for use in language programmes.

5

Integrating video into the language programme

So far we have discussed what there is in the way of video equipment and materials and we have looked at how we can use the machine. It's time now to turn our attention to how video can fit into our teaching as a whole. This chapter examines reasons for using video in language teaching and considers when and how we could introduce it into the syllabus and into the lesson.

What does video contribute?

Video is not the only resource we have at our disposal in the language classroom. It takes its place among a range of other aids we use quite regularly, so we have to decide what its strengths are. What does it do particularly well in the context of language teaching?

It presents realistic 'slices of life'

If your students want to study spoken English, you will spend part of the time in the classroom working on examples of the spoken language. Most language courses use dialogue or a narrative to present the language of the unit. We use examples in the textbook, and often on audio, which gives them the greater realism of different voices and sound effects. When, with video, we can add moving pictures to the soundtrack, the examples of language in use become even more realistic. These examples are more comprehensive too, because they put before us the ways people communicate visually as well as verbally. So video is a good means of bringing 'slices of living language' into the classroom.

It gets students talking

In many language classrooms today there are times when we want to get our students talking — to us and to each other. We want to give them the opportunity to put their own language into practice in a genuine effort to communicate. So we look for situations where our learners will really have something they want to say to each other. The right video material can do this in a range of ways: its vivid presentation of settings and characters can be used to set the scene for roleplay; it can present a case with such impact that it sparks off fierce debate; we all make our own interpretations of what we see and so video can be a stimulus to genuine communication in the classroom by bringing out different opinions within the group.

It provides visual support

We all send and receive visual signals when we talk to each other. These help us decipher what is being communicated. It must therefore help learners when they listen to a foreign language if they can see as well as hear what is going on. And video's moving pictures also help learners concentrate because they provide a focus of attention while they listen. Both these forms of support suggest that video is a good medium for extended listening to the foreign language. The more exposure learners have to the language, the better they are likely to learn it. In some situations, the classroom is the only place learners can hear the foreign language spoken, so video becomes a means of giving them a 'language bath' in the classroom.

It offers variety and entertainment

In our homes we associate the small screen with entertainment. We expect to enjoy the experience of viewing. Learners bring the same expectations to the experience of viewing video in the classroom and we can encourage this positive attitude by using video in a flexible way. It is a medium of great variety, with a wealth of different kinds of software which we can use to ring the changes in our teaching. This book suggests many ways in which we can use video in a different way to viewing television. We can also at times use it just like television. Video helps us provide a richer and more varied language environment within which learning can take place. The combination of variety, interest and entertainment we can derive from video makes it an aid which can help develop motivation in learners.

Planning video into the syllabus

The integration of video into your syllabus will depend on the kind of video installation you have. If you have video playback available in your classroom whenever you want it, along with a good choice of materials, you can afford to use it in a variety of ways. In some lessons you might use it for five minutes. In others it could be the springboard for a two-hour session. If you only have access to the machine once a month in a special video room, you will want to make it the centre of attention for that session. Whatever access you have, it is much better to plan video sessions into the syllabus. If it is left as an optional extra, it's too easy to forget about it or to decide not to bother. It helps everyone get started if there are notes indicating where and how video materials would fit into the syllabus.

On what basis can this syllabus integration be organised? There isn't always an obvious link between the materials you have and the syllabus in use.

Links through language items

The link through language is the most obvious and most straightforward one to make if your syllabus is based on linguistic items such as language structures or functions. Published materials for ELT normally reflect trends in language teaching and the current language-focussed series can generally be linked to the syllabus through the language functions or structures they present.

. In non-ELT materials you can look for situations which are likely to feature highly predictable language: scenes set in restaurants or shops, at parties, the reception desk or the dining table can sometimes be picked out of a longer programme and used in isolation to give an example of particular language functions in operation. (However you might be surprised at how often these settings don't include the language you expect to hear.)

Once you've found a video sequence you could use to present specific language items, you then have to decide when you will introduce it in your teaching of a unit. There are several possibilities:

— it could be used to present language — either for the introduction of new areas of language or to supplement what has been taught by other means and methods;

— it could be used to check whether students are already familiar with the language and can use it confidently, to help the teacher diagnose problems;

— it could be used to stimulate learners to produce the language themselves through roleplay or discussion.

We return to these uses in the last part of this chapter, when we look in detail at roles for video in the lesson.

Links through topics

Topics are a feature of some language syllabuses. A unit of work might be based around a topic like ecology or the leisure interests of young people in Britain or the education systems of different countries. A video programme about the same topic could be a welcome addition to that unit. It could put a different perspective on the topic; it could introduce new information; it could invite comparison of the ways the same subject can be treated in different media or from different points of view.

Another way of linking through topic is by means of subject matter introduced in the textbook for language practice. For example, talking about the jobs people do is often used to practise describing daily routines. There may be video materials on your shelves showing people at work which you could use to extend practice of this kind. An exercise in describing places could be based on a video sequence which showed a particular town. All of this uses video to introduce variety and interest to classroom work.

Links through activities

Your syllabus may include slots for the development of certain skills such as listening to lectures or writing reports. You could think of using video material occasionally as an input to these activities. A video recording of a meeting could give practice in taking notes of main points. A documentary programme could form the basis for discussion in the weekly slot for communicative activities. Viewing an interesting story requires the exercise of listening skills.

The 'video slot'

You do not always have to have a specific link to other items on the syllabus. Some sets of video material are self-contained and come with their own activities: a serial story, a training series for management skills, a set of business meetings. Any of these could create their own regular slot on the timetable: a Sherlock Holmes story once a month, perhaps, or a weekly session for the Business English group to view the next episode of *Bid for Power*. Alternatively a range of different video materials could be used in a period earmarked for video. The important thing is that the slot be timetabled in, so that even where video provision is very limited, everyone is encouraged to think about how they can use what there is.

Integrating video into the lesson

This brings us on to thinking about how you can integrate video into your lesson. The rest of this chapter looks at how you might do this, using examples from a range of video materials, ELT and non-ELT. The Video Plans in this chapter are taken from Teacher's Guides and other print support produced for published video materials. Although the suggestions are for a specific piece of video, they have been selected because the ideas are transferrable to other materials.

Using materials which focus on language

Is video better suited to one stage of a lesson rather than another? With materials designed to highlight language items, we have an indication of how materials designers approach the question of video's role in the lesson. I will look at this in relation to the traditional stages of a language lesson, presentation, practice, reinforcement, and to the elicitation stage some teachers introduce before presentation.

(a) Video for elicitation

There are times when you want to encourage talk within the classroom group, with students drawing on their own language resources to express thoughts they want to communicate. There are also times when you need to find out how much your students know or can do with language. You may have a new group for whom you have to work out a syllabus, or you may want to check to see whether a revision session is necessary or not. For all of these reasons you may want to hear your students talking with as little prompting as possible from you. Students often find that their ability to produce language which is appropriate for a particular situation is less than they had expected. The technique of getting them to supply the missing dialogue after a silent viewing of a scene provides a good opportunity for you and them to find out what language they have at their command and how flexibly they can use it. When this is your purpose you might use a short sequence for as little as five or ten minutes at the beginning of a lesson.

(b) Video at the presentation stage

In a sense all video material is presenting examples of language. I use the term here in the language teaching sense of the presentation of new language items which will be the focus for the next unit of work. How appropriate is video for this stage of a unit? In language teaching we are accustomed to using dialogues which present very restricted examples of language. This is acceptable in the textbook, and can even be made to work on audio, but it is more difficult when we can see real people in a real setting on video. The scene looks awkward and unconvincing if the language is so controlled and repetitive that the interaction becomes quite unnatural. Because of this the language in video materials, even for elementary level, tends to be a little more varied than it would be in the textbook. Most ELT series are intended to supplement what is in the textbook not to replace it and they are intended to be used to consolidate the learning of language that has already been presented in another form.

The *Follow Me* course is one which does aim to introduce new language items through video. This is done within the programme itself by using very restricted examples of language and by recycling these examples through the programme and through the course in a range of different short scenes. The fact that *Follow Me* was designed for broadcast meant that it had to do its own presentation, as it were, for home viewers. A teacher with a video machine in the classroom has the choice of when to use video material and could for example use a sequence with an appropriate setting to establish a context before new language items are introduced.

It's very unlikely that video will be your only means of presenting language so you do have a choice. Assuming that all the materials you have are equally suitable for your students, the main distinguishing feature of the video materials is likely to be that they provide the most realistic examples of the language in use. Your choice therefore could be boiled down to whether you want to start with the 'real thing' on video, as an example of what the unit is about, or whether you want to keep the most realistic example for later, to reinforce what has gone before.

(c) Video used for reinforcement

This is a good use of video because it capitalises on video's naturalism to present more realistic examples of language, and the visual support video offers can lighten the additional language load. Video Plan 6 on page 53 is taken from materials intended to be used as language reinforcement.

In this treatment a variety of techniques is used to elicit the language learners already know before they reach the 'View, Listen and Compare' stage. By then, known items have been recycled and summarised and any new ways of asking permission in the sequence can be highlighted. A lesson of this kind would be appropriate as the final stage in a unit of work on ways of asking permission. It could also be a revision session.

VIDEO PLAN 6: Using video for reinforcement (1)

(From *Video English*)

VIDEOSCRIPT

Time
0.00 A woman carrying a tray with food on it, approaches a man sitting at a table in a crowded canteen.

0.04 Woman: Hello. May I join you?
  Man: Mm. Please do.

The woman puts her tray on the table. She goes to the next table to get a chair.

0.09 Woman: Do you mind if I take this chair?
  Second woman: Somebody's sitting there actually.
  Woman: Oh.

She goes to another table.

0.15 Woman: Could I take this chair?
  Second man: Please.

The woman takes the chair and then sits down.

0.22 Man: So how are you?
  Woman: Fine, and you?
  Man: Yes, very well.

0.26 End of sequence.

TEACHING SUGGESTIONS

Stage One: Defining the context — what is happening?

1. Play the first section (0.00 to 0.04) **with sound only**, up to the part where the woman begins to speak. T asks SS to listen to the sound and then guess where they are.

  Where are they?

2. Play the first section (0.00 to 0.04) **with picture and sound**. Did SS guess correctly?

3. T asks SS to predict what is going to happen next. If necessary T asks prompt questions:

  Is she going to sit down?
  Where?
  Where will she put her tray?

Stage Two: Predicting the language — what are they saying?

1. View **without sound** until where the woman puts her tray on the table (0.00 to 0.07). T asks SS:

  What did she say?
  What did the man say?
  Does she know him?

T asks SS in pairs to guess the dialogue and make notes of their guesses.

2. View **without sound** until where the woman puts her hands on the chair at the other table (0.07 to 0.10).

  What did she say?

3. T asks SS to predict what is going to happen.

  What is the second woman going to say?
SS offers suggestions.

4. View next section **without sound** until where the woman moves to the next table (0.10 to 0.14). T asks SS:

  Were you correct?
  What did the second woman say?

5. View final section **without sound**. T asks SS:

  What did she say to the second man?
  What did he say to her?

6. Replay the whole sequence **without sound**. T asks SS in groups of four to perform their predictions of the whole dialogue.

Stage Three: Summarising the language

1. T summarises on the board, possible ways of asking and giving permission. For example:

  Can I ...?
  Could I ...?
  May I ...?
  Is it alright if I ...?

2. SS practise these structures by asking each other if they can borrow a book, a pen, a chair, etc.

Stage Four: View, listen and compare

1. Replay the whole sequence **with sound**. T asks SS to look and listen in order to compare what they hear, with their own guesses. Who guessed correctly?

2. Replay the whole sequence again, pausing to ask comprehension questions. For example:

  Why can't she take the first chair?

If necessary replay **with sound only** for intensive listening to parts of the dialogue.

3. To aid comprehension T gives SS a gapped videoscript. In pairs, SS listen to the sound only and try to fill gaps.

Stage Five: Acting the scene

1. SS act out the sequence in groups of four. T monitors the groups and corrects the language and pronunciation if necessary. T chooses one or two groups to provide a model to the other SS.

2. After acting out the sequence T asks SS to act out similar but not identical situations eg:

  You are in a train. Ask if you can sit in an empty seat.
  You are in a canteen. You need some salt. Ask somebody at the next table.
  You want to use somebody's telephone.

What proportion of class time should it take up? We are always interested to know how much classwork any material can generate. It's a factor in assessing value for money and we also need to have some idea of how the material will fit into our normal teaching pattern.

Most of the suggestions made in Teacher's Notes that accompany ELT video materials would lead to a full lesson built round each video unit. The way the video fits into the lesson varies from one publication to another. In Video Plan 6 we have an example of very intensive treatment of a very short sequence (26 seconds) where the video is repeatedly returned to as a stimulus to another activity. Its use is woven through the bulk of the lesson. Video Plan 7 illustrates a different approach to a longer sequence (about 15

VIDEO PLAN 7: Using video for reinforcement (2)

(From *Family Affair*)

VIEWING TASK

1. How many times does Anna use the phone?
2. Does Jeff have a television in his study?

CHECK

Answer True or False.

1. Anna and Jim discuss the problems of the heating.
2. Anna phones the office about the plumbing.
3. Jim asks Jeff how he travelled there.
4. Jeff makes two phone calls.
5. Jeff has got a new manager for the shop.
6. Jim lets Anna make coffee.
7. Jim wants to lock up the site office.
8. Anna says Terry is with his father on a boat.
9. Jeff's home in New Zealand is very modern.
10. His study has a desk, a sofa and a record player.
11. He likes to be alone in his study.
12. Jeff says that he is married.

TALK ABOUT THE STORY

1. Do you think that Anna and Jeff's requests are reasonable?
2. How would you describe Jim's attitude: rude, polite, or businesslike?
3. Why does Anna have 'a feeling' about a wife back home in New Zealand?

FOCUS

What was the question?

1. JIM: Are you...too?
   JEFF: No, I'm just here for the ride.

2. JEFF: It's funny to think someone ..., isn't it?
   ANNA: Why funny? It's just a house now. It takes people to make it into a home.

3. ANNA: Is that ...?
   JEFF: That's where I hide away.

4. JEFF: Who said ...?
   ANNA: It's just a feeling I have, that's all.

Complete the conversations.

Anna and Jeff each make two requests for permission in the site manager's office.

1. ANNA: ... phone?
   JIM: Yeah, ...

2. JEFF: ... phone?
   JIM: Yes, ...

3. ANNA: ... coffee, Jim?
   JIM: Sorry, but ...

4. JEFF: ... again?
   JIM: Well, actually, I'm ...

The remaining six exercises do not refer back to the video sequence.

minutes). Here the viewing of the sequence is used as a springboard for a set of activities which follow it. Most of these refer back to the content of the video but repeat viewing is not suggested.

Let's Watch returns to a viewing of the whole sequence at several points in the suggested sequence of activities. Each unit also includes a second, silent sequence, which provides a basis for exploitation of language presented earlier in the unit. Video Plan 8 is taken from the Teacher's Notes and suggests several ways of treating a short silent sequence of about two minutes.

VIDEO PLAN 8: Using video for reinforcement (3)
(From *Let's Watch*)

You can use the silent sequences in several ways:

(a) (i) Play the sequence to the class and pause at various points.
     (ii) When you pause, ask the students to guess what will happen next.

(b) (i) Play the sequence without pausing.
     (ii) Ask the students in groups to discuss what they have seen and try to reconstruct the story of the events in order.
     (iii) Replay the story at the end of the discussion to check the reconstruction. (This uses the sequence as a basis for a report or testimony of what happened. It usually promotes lively discussion when each group reports, as different people will recall different things.)

(c) (i) Play the sequence several times and ask students to focus on the points of the sequence where people appear to be talking to each other. They must watch carefully and imagine what the people are saying.
     (ii) Then, working in pairs, the students can make up a dialogue.
     (iii) The students can either speak or record their dialogue to match the speakers' actions on the video.

     (If you have a double audio track on your machine, some of the pairs of students can record their dialogue on the second track so that it seems as if the people on the screen are talking. Alternatively, the students can try speaking along with the sequence.)

(d) (i) Play the sequence several times.
     (ii) Ask students to write a commentary on the events, similar to a sports commentary.
     (iii) Ask students to speak their commentary as the sequence is played, or they can record it as in (c) above.

Video for language practice

I interpret 'practice' in its broad sense of the practice of a range of skills. This section looks at examples of different types of skills practice suggested for video materials.

(a) Use of visual prompts
Several video workbooks for students feature still pictures taken from the video sequence. They are sometimes used for previewing activity, or they

can be used as recall devices for language study and practice as they are in the 'Focus' section of *Family Affair* (see Video Plan 7) and in the example in Video Plan 9.

VIDEO PLAN 9: Video-related activities (1)

(From *Follow Me to San Francisco*)

Read and match

Look at the pictures.
Read the expressions at the right-hand side of the page and match them to the pictures.
Discuss your choices with your teacher and compare them with the choices of your classmates.

(a) Oh, what a shame!
(b) Oh, I can't believe we're here already.
(c) I'd like to give you a little something.
(d) Oh no, ma'am. That's okay. Really.
(e) You new in town?
(f) You'd better come with me.

1.

2.

3.

If you don't have still pictures for the video materials you are using, you could still adapt these ideas by using freeze frame on the video itself. With videodisc it is possible to select the frame precisely and speedily so that a set of stills on the screen could very easily be used.

Video Plan 10 gives two further ideas for tasks which exploit the visual element of the sequence as it is played.

VIDEO PLAN 10: Video-related activities (2)

(From *Video English*)

Optional Extension Activities

1. T lists the following items on the board:

lifebuoy	lock-gate	barge	headscarf
swimming steps	railings	rail	wrapping paper

   Replay the whole sequence and ask SS to say where the items are.

2. ASKING QUESTIONS T writes the following words or phrases on the board and explains that they are the **answers** to possible questions about the sequence. T plays the sequence again **with sound** and asks SS in pairs to form the questions. For example, the question for the first answer might be: 'Where are they walking?'

By a canal	Because he is worried about getting fat
Some chocolate	Across the bridge
Yes. She does	

(b) Roleplay

This activity is suggested with several sets of material and at different stages in the video-based lesson. In Video Plan 6 we saw roleplay introduced after silent viewing and before students listened to the dialogue. It was suggested again as a final recap of the video sequence. You can also stop the tape at a dramatic point in a story and ask your students to devise their own ending to it. Several teacher's books suggest a final move away from the situation portrayed on the video to other, similar situations.

(c) Video drills

Some video materials have a practice stage built into each unit. The course *It's Your Turn To Speak* uses laboratory drill techniques, with gaps left for the student to supply parts of the dialogue. The camera leads the viewer into the scene and a symbol appears on the screen as a prompt for the viewer to speak. *Let's Watch* includes video exercises which are similar to traditional audio-cued drills. The *Follow Me* guide suggests the use of a VCR similar to the use we sometimes make of audiocassette players in the classroom: the 'listen and repeat' technique of pausing the machine after each utterance for students to repeat it. This is simply using your control of the machine and could be applied to any video material.

(d) Comprehension exercises

Comprehension is involved when we look at video and so the techniques for developing and checking comprehension with audio or print are equally valid for video. The examples we have seen include multiple choice and true/false questions, gap-filling tasks, re-ordering jumbled sentences, filling in information on worksheets. All of them treat the video sequence simply as another form of text and are familiar exercise types. This is a useful reminder that video is just another aid at your disposal. Even if you are new to it, you probably already have a range of ideas for language work which could perfectly well apply to video.

Materials which present topics

We turn now from materials with a focus on language to materials you choose because of the topic they present. This could include ELT and non-ELT material and will mostly consist of documentary programmes or extracts from current affairs programmes. Topic-based programmes present information and opinions. You can use them to stimulate discussion, or as sources of data for tasks or projects.

(a) Collecting information

An information-gathering task serves the purpose of directing viewing. This is a good activity for small group project work as it lends itself to the pooling of information and sharing different elements of the task. Video Plan 11 is drawn from worksheets prepared for Danish teenagers to use with a programme from a Thames Television series: *The John Smith Show*. This series took four British families, all with the surname Smith, and used it to look at aspects of life in contemporary Britain.

VIDEO PLAN 11: Using video as a source of information (1)

(From *The John Smith Show*)

THE SMITHS AT WORK

FAMILY 1

You are now going to watch the episode about the Smiths' jobs - <u>without</u> the soundtrack.

So watch carefully. The recorder will be stopped after each person's presentation of his/her job. Be prepared to answer the following questions. If there's not room enough - ask your teacher for a sheet of paper.

What's John's job?
Why do you think so?
What's Jennifer's job?
Why do you think so?
What do you think Jennifer and her daughter are talking about on the phone?

Now watch the episode about <u>JOBS</u> again. This time with the soundtrack. Fill in this worksheet and answer the questions.

FAMILY 1	JOB TITLE	FIRM
JOHN		
JENNIFER		

1. Do you think John likes his job? Why?

2. Do you think Jennifer likes her job. Why?

3. Why are the children phoning Jennifer at work?

WHAT WE EARN

What do you think these people could expect to earn in your country per month? What do you think the Smiths' earn? Fill in the following.

JOB	Pay in Denmark		Pay in Britain	
	£	d.kr.	£	d.kr.
bus conductor				
cheque processor				
wood model maker				
prod.control analyst				
vet				
prim.school teacher				

When you have watched the programme, fill in the rest of this worksheet with some of the answers you'll get in the programme, the rest you are going to find out yourself by doing a bit of arithmetic.

(Only part of the unit is reproduced here)

VIDEO PLAN 12: Using video as a source of information (2)

(From *Television English*)

The following sections are common to most, but not all, units:

Before you watch

This section introduces the topic by setting a puzzle, a quiz, or a discussion which involves guessing or predicting, using illustrations as clues. These activities allow students to find out and use essential new vocabulary as well as giving background information about the topic.

Watch and decide

This consists of a range of activities in which students watch the picture without listening to the soundtrack, and get
— training in interpreting visual clues to meaning
— a chance to predict the language that they will hear later.

Listen and draw / check / compare

These are activities where the students listen to the soundtrack without the picture. They provide
— practice in careful listening for meaning
— a chance to check predictions made earlier.

View and check

In this activity students watch the picture *and* listen to the soundtrack. It follows the previous two types of activity and, besides enabling students to check their answers or solutions, it helps them focus on the language used, and to link the spoken word with the picture on the screen.

Viewing tasks

Students watch the picture and listen to the sound and tackle a range of tasks which involve intensive study of the meanings and messages of specific parts of the television extracts.

Television English also applies classroom techniques to off-air material. The Teacher's Notes suggest a variety of activities which take learners back to the video 'text' several times. Video Plan 12 above, from the introduction to the book, gives a summary of the most common activities.

(b) Debating a topic

Choose a topic which you know will interest and involve your students. If possible it should also be a topic about which your class will have differing views. Video Plan 13 shows how topic-based material can slot into debate which takes place before and after the viewing.

VIDEO PLAN 13: Using video to stimulate debate

(From *Video English*)

STAGE ONE: PREPARING TO VIEW

1. T explains that SS are going to see a sequence of a committee meeting trying to decide how to conduct an anti-smoking campaign. In particular, the committee has to decide on the design for a poster.

2. T divides the class into four groups, and tells each group that they are going to focus on one of the characters in the sequence. At this point T should not tell SS either the name or the sex of their character.

3. **Previewing task** T gives the four groups one of the following role-cards:

Group A

You chair the meeting. You inform the others that the purpose of the meeting is to decide how to spend five thousand pounds on an anti-smoking campaign. You tell the others how you wish to conduct the meeting.

Group B

You think the campaign should stress the *positive* aspects of *not* smoking. What points do you make?

Group C

You think the campaign should stress the *negative* and harmful aspects of smoking. What points do you make?

Group D

You think the campaign should stress that it is anti-social to smoke in public. What points do you make?

Each group makes a list of the points they would make at the meeting. (Group A decides how they would open the meeting, and how they would conduct it.) T helps SS and provides vocabulary where necessary.

4. **Roleplay** Each group elects a representative to take part in a roleplay of the meeting in front of the class. Each representative makes the points that his or her group has decided upon. The representative from Group A chairs the meeting and controls the discussion. T takes note of any language errors, and draws attention to them after the roleplay.

STAGE TWO: SCENE ONE

1. **Viewing tasks** T explains to SS that their tasks while viewing Scene One are:
   (a) identify their group's character
   (b) assess his or her personality
   (c) compare the points he or she makes, with the group's list of points
   (d) assess his or her attitude to the other characters.

2. **Silent viewing** View the first section of Scene One without sound (0.00 to 1.20) until where Jill is speaking. SS, in groups, try to identify which is their character. When trying to identify, T asks SS to focus on the descriptions of the characters' clothes.

3. **Viewing with sound** View enough of the sequence from the beginning, with sound, until each group has identified their character. (NB Group D should be able to deduce who their character is even before he speaks, simply by a process of elimination.) Before continuing, T can clarify the characters on the board:

   Group A: Mary (chairperson)
   Group B: Jill (positive approach)
   Group C: Ian (shock tactics)
   Group D: Anthony (anti-social habit)

Now view the whole of Scene One with sound. Each group performs the viewing tasks, taking notes on their character's personality, the points he or she makes, and on his or her attitude to the others. After viewing, each group discusses their character, and the notes they have made. Then each group summarises the results of their viewing tasks and presents them to the rest of the class.

4. **Discussion** T discusses with the class the way each character behaves in Scene One. Did they all behave well? Did the chairperson run the meeting well? Whose opinions do SS agree with?

STAGE THREE: SCENE TWO
(as for Stage Two: Scene One)

STAGE FOUR: FOLLOW-UP ACTIVITIES

1. **Focus on non-verbal communication** T plays the whole sequence, but pauses to freeze frame at each of the following points to ask SS to explain the meaning of the features of non-verbal communication which take place (gestures, facial expression, posture):

   0.46 Why does Jill lean forward?
   1.06 What does Jill's sign mean?
   1.20 What does Ian's posture suggest?
   1.35 Why does Anthony raise his hand?
   1.37 Why does Mary nod?
   1.47 Why does Anthony shift his position?

(Only part of the unit is reproduced here)

(c) Producing a commentary

Video Plan 14 is taken from a course developed in the Free University of Berlin which used a range of texts drawn from different media. These were grouped according to theme and accompanied by a variety of tasks. This is one example of a task related to an extract from off-air documentary material within a unit on drugs.

VIDEO PLAN 14: Producing a commentary

(From *An Intensive Theme-Oriented Course in Advanced English for First-Semester German University Students of Diverse Subject Studies*)

Topic

'Everyday drugs': alcohol

Text

An extract from a television documentary about the problem of alcohol in society.

Aims

To give students practice in making suggestions and responding to the suggestions of others, in writing to inform, and in presenting a brief written statement orally.

Procedure

Students see a brief excerpt from a television film in which the picture illustrates the commentary. This is first shown without the soundtrack. On the basis of the picture alone, they make notes of the aspects of the problem handled. A second showing of the same excerpt enables them to amplify their notes.

Students then form groups of four or five and collaborate on the writing of a commentary on the basis of the following instructions:

WRITING A COMMENTARY — small group work

The following words are included in the commentary to the excerpt:

off-licence: Br. Eng. (in this text) a licence permitting a store to sell sealed bottles of liquor, but not allowing drinking on the premises, or the sale of individual drinks (The Random House Dictionary of the English Language)

booze: sl. (in this text) alcoholic drink (Longman Dictionary of Contemporary English)

housekeeping: (in this text) an amount of money set aside each week or month by the husband and/or wife to pay for food or other things needed in the home (based on the Longman Dictionary of Contemporary English.)

In your group, write a short commentary covering all the points that the group's members have picked up from the pictures and including the above words. (The original commentary had seven sentences. Your own should not be longer.)

The excerpt may be shown again if the groups wish it. Each group's finished script is checked by the teacher, who marks any mistakes or awkwardnesses and returns the script to the group concerned for correction and improvement, only providing these him/herself in the last resort.

The commentaries are then recorded, the following procedure being followed:

RECORDING THE COMMENTARY

Choose a member of your group to record the commentary. The chosen person should rehearse his/her reading with the help of the group before making the recording. The recorded commentaries produced by your own and other groups will then be played alongside the silent videotext.

(Only part of the unit is reproduced here)

Video materials as examples of communication

A different approach to video materials is to look at how they communicate their message. This is particularly relevant to non-ELT materials since they were produced to convey a message to a particular audience. They can be studied as examples of uses of the medium in the context of the society that produced them. In language programmes which include an element of project work and with students who are interested in contemporary issues, this flavour of media studies can be very motivating.

VIDEO PLAN 15: Students produce their own scripts

(From *Television English*: Sparrows of St James's)

ALTERNATIVE A: WRITE A SCRIPT

The existing sound script for this programme is by David Attenborough, a well-known TV personality. However, his script will almost certainly be too difficult for students in a class lower than you to understand. The purpose of this task is for you, as a class, to prepare and record a simple script that other students could follow more easily.

1. Watch the whole sequence without sound. Decide what the message could be at each stage.

2. Decide where to subdivide the sequence, for example, where you think a natural break occurs, where a new theme begins. You will probably find three fairly equal sections. Now work in groups, each taking one section of the sequence.

3. Read the Vision script and then watch the sequence, again without sound, pausing to match the Vision script to the video at each stage.

4. In groups, plan a simple Sound script for your section. See the sample script below. Remember you will have to read your script out loud, so time your reading to fit in with the vision. You do not need to speak all the time; sometimes, the pictures speak for themselves and silence is best.

5. If you really cannot understand what the theme of your section is, you could refer to the David Attenborough script. But remember, this will have to be simplified a lot.

6. Finally, record your script on audio cassette. Do this while watching the sequence, so you synchronise the sound with the vision. Take turns to read; change 'presenters' when there is a natural break. Have a practice run through before recording.

7. Replay the video and your tape recording together and check that they correspond.

8. Now listen to David Attenborough's version and compare.

Sample Sound Script

The original sound script begins like this: 'Cheerful, lively, full of fun, the familiar House Sparrow has many friends.'

You may of course choose your own opening words.

(Only part of the unit is reproduced here)

ALTERNATIVE B: PLAN THE VISION

Note: you may find it easier to make a photocopy of the Sound script with just *one* column on the left of each page, so that you can write the Vision script beside it.

1. Read the Sound script and discuss in small groups what should be shown on the screen. For each column of script, aim at an average of about 10 to 12 different camera shots. Remember that there may be gaps where there are no words spoken, but where different pictures are still being shown. Look at the list of different types of camera shots on the Introductory page, and decide which would be best for each sentence or group of sentences.

2. Each small group should tell the class what they have decided, and try to decide the best way to make a Vision script to match the Sound script.

3. Divide the sequence into sections, one section for each small group. Each group should write, in note form, a description of the camera shots for their section. See sample Vision script below.

4. Watch the video sequence without sound, once or twice, to see how your ideas for camera shots compare with the original film.

5. Finally, view the whole programme, with sound, and evaluate it. Where do you think your ideas might have been more effective (for example for an audience from your country?) Where do you think David Attenborough did better than you? How far did you get the same or similar shots?

6. If you wish, you could now look at the original Vision script to see how it was done by the BBC.

Sample Vision Script

CU Sparrow, perched on gate, singing.

MLS Sparrow flying from gate. Buckingham Palace in background.

MS Sparrow on perch on railing

S/imposed SPARROWS OF ST JAMES'S

MS Soldiers parading in front of Buckingham Palace, pull out to show people watching them.

All film, video and television production is an example of the use of tools other than language to communicate to an audience. One way of analysing video programmes is to look at the film techniques employed: editing decisions, camera angles, the way images are juxtaposed all have an effect on the viewer, who is often unaware of it.

The group tasks in Video Plan 15 on page 62 encourage students to think about the way a programme was put together.

A study of this kind can be related to texts in other media too, giving a comparison of, for example, different ways of approaching the same topic. The treatment of off-air material outlined in Video Plans 14 and 15 could form the basis for discussion of this kind.

Using video materials which tell stories

There are three things to look for in a story: the characters, the plot and the style of telling the story. This is a useful basis for thinking about how you could use a story in class. You will certainly want to make sure your students can follow the plot, and an appreciation of the characters is usually very closely linked to our understanding of a plot. How far you discuss the style will depend on the interests of your students.

Interesting stories are good material for developing the skill of gist listening. You can set a clear goal: the ability to retell the main elements of the plot. It is usually possible to follow the plot without understanding every word in the story and you can choose stories on video which have a strong visual contribution to the storyline. Look particularly for information about characters: attitudes are often indicated by facial expressions or movements. Below is an example of the way you could organise your notes as you preview a story.

VERBAL INFORMATION i.e. content of conversations; names of characters etc.	VISUAL INFORMATION appearance; setting; attitudes	PREVIEW QUESTIONS who? what? why? where?	POSTVIEW QUESTIONS questions on detail or to elicit views on the story

These notes would help you prepare a lesson of the kind outlined in Video Plan 16 on page 64.

VIDEO PLAN 16: Viewing a story

(From *Sherlock Holmes and Dr Watson*)

To establish characters

Before viewing give the class the names of the characters who will appear in the scene. Their task as they view is to identify these characters, to note points about their appearance and characters and to collect information about the part they play in the story. You could use a worksheet like this:

NAME (Supplied by teacher)	DESCRIPTION (What they look like, how they dress)	ROLE IN STORY (What they do)

With the first story you use, the opening title sequence could be used to identify Sherlock Holmes, Dr Watson and Inspector Lestrade, the three characters who appear in each story. Start by checking whether anyone in the group knows anything of the Sherlock Holmes stories and build up any information the class can give you. Put the class in groups and assign each group one of the characters. After viewing the title sequence the groups have to say which was their character. (Lestrade is identified by name, the other two are not.)

As they watch the story, they can add to the information they have about the character, gradually developing a character sketch of each one.

To establish plot

Basic questions to ask yourself about any sequence in the stories:

What was the most important thing that happened in that scene?
What information did I get from that scene?

Decide from your own viewing what you think the answers should be and then guide your students towards these points by the questions you set. You should always set one or two central **previewing questions** before each section, which then become comprehension questions after viewing.

A similar organisation of student notes, based on Teacher's Notes for *Bid for Power* is shown in Video Plan 17.

VIDEO PLAN 17: Viewing a story

(From *Bid for Power*)

Students can make a record of what happens in the video story. A simple way of doing this is to fill in the details of each scene on a sheet of paper divided into three columns headed WHERE (the country and location), WHO (the characters) and WHAT (the topic of the scene).

You may find it useful for your students to keep other notes, especially on the background to the story. For instance, they can build up files on Tanaku (its economy, politics, etc.), the firms involved in bidding for the silicon project (Pansil, Faulkner Enterprises etc.) and the main characters in the story.

Using materials
which focus on
cultural features

· The camera can take us into people's homes and lives and places of work and lay before us evidence of what life and work is like in another country. You would probably choose to use materials of this kind because the aspects of the culture featured are of relevance to your students. Perhaps they are soon to go to Britain or the States to study or as tourists. Or perhaps they are working in Britain and having to interpret the culture that is all around them. If these are your reasons for using video material which highlights aspects of a society, use the video to find out what your students want to know about it.

Different people will notice different things and some of them may surprise you. Leave it as open as possible and encourage them to ask questions, by setting preview questions such as 'What differences do you notice between British/North American customs and those of your own country?' 'Does anything seem strange to you in the scene?'

Video or audio?

We said at the beginning of this chapter that you would have to choose when to use video rather than another classroom aid. It's fairly clear when you would use a book or an Overhead Projector or a magazine picture in your teaching and it's not difficult to see that video makes a different contribution. The aid that we are most likely to use for the same reasons as video is the audio tape or cassette recorder. We are accustomed to using audio to present examples of language in use. It lets us bring into the classroom different voices and different accents and a skilful use of sound effects can suggest a setting. We can do all of these things better with video. So, if we had the same range of materials on video as we do on audio, would we continue to use audio in language teaching? The answer is yes, but it would have a more limited role. It would be limited to the function it is most useful for in the language classroom: intensive listening.

We have established that video is a good medium to use for extensive listening. It is not however so well suited to an intensive, detailed study of spoken language. The present generation of videocassette machines does not respond speedily or accurately to the stop, rewind, replay sequence you go through in intensive listening to identify every word. There is the added irritation of having the picture interfered with and the screen takes a moment to settle down after a restart. If you want your students to listen intensively to a dialogue, don't do it on video. The ideal would be to have the soundtrack on an audio cassette. Then, after using it on video, any intensive listening tasks could be carried out on audio. Where this is not possible, it is best not to attempt intensive listening. You don't need to treat every dialogue in the same way anyway, so keep that kind of work for audio materials and try to use video for the work it is best suited for.

6

Making full use of your video

There is no one right way to use video in the classroom. There are as many right ways as there are effective uses of video to assist the learning of a language. Complex media like video have an aura of mystery about them. *We* put it there. The electronics of the machinery *are* complex. Professional production requires specialist skills. It is easy to get teaching materials wrong, difficult to get them right. But you as a teacher in the classroom with your own learners and your own objectives can take all of that for granted. You have a tool at your disposal which is simple to operate. You know what materials you have to select from. Explore the different ways you can use them. Don't let anyone persuade you that there are rules about using video that you mustn't break.

And there are people who sincerely believe that rules exist. Who argue that, because television makes its effect through the continuous screening of moving pictures, the flow of a programme must not be interrupted when it is shown on video. Or that it is wrong to take an excerpt from a programme and look at it in isolation. There is no research to prove any of this one way or the other. Any use of any resource in education is only right or wrong in relation to its success or failure in helping people learn. And until there is evidence to prove any of these claims it is best to try to make your own judgement of whether a method works or does not work with your learners.

This chapter goes more deeply into what video offers and how we might use it. It ends with a look at uses appropriate to learning objectives at different levels.

Exploiting the visual

Think of the different ways you can transmit a message to another human being: by waving, nodding, banging on the neighbour's wall, writing a letter, frowning, slamming the door, moving away from someone who sits beside you, pointing, raising your eyebrows.

All of this is in addition to, and often accompanying, speech.

Look at this script of a typical 'Introductions and greetings' dialogue:

John and Mary are sitting at a table in a cafe. Bill comes in and looks round. John beckons him over.
JOHN: Hi Bill.
He points to a chair.
Join us.
BILL: Thanks.
He sits down, smiles at Mary. She doesn't smile back.

JOHN: Oh, you haven't met Mary have you?
BILL: No I haven't.
Stretches out his hand to Mary.
Hullo Mary. Pleased to meet you.
JOHN: This is my good friend Bill. We were at school together.
Mary didn't expect him to shake hands and is a bit slow in putting out her hand.
MARY: Hullo.

In this encounter the language communicates greetings, introduction, invitation and information. One gesture — indicating the chair — supplements the language it accompanies; the other — the handshake — is a social convention. The smiles — or lack of them — probably tell Bill and Mary something about their attitudes to each other or to the situation they find themselves in. They should be picking up other clues about each other too: the accents they speak with, the way they are dressed, the kind of hairstyles they have all tell us something about people we meet. As viewers of this scene we could also have deduced something about the relationship between John and Mary from the way they were sitting together and the way they looked at each other. We wouldn't have found it difficult to reconstruct the exchange even if we had been too far away to hear what was said.

All of this is a reminder that many messages are conveyed simultaneously when human beings communicate 'face to face'. Some of these messages are intentional — when John speaks to Bill he chooses language, makes deliberate gestures and controls the expression on his face in a conscious attempt to signal certain information and attitudes. If John and Bill have a lot in common — if, for example, they come from the same community or are part of the same culture — then Bill is likely to interpret most of the signals in the way John intended. However misinterpretation is always possible and it is also very possible that Bill is picking up other signals about John which John is not aware he's sending.

The ways in which we communicate in face-to-face interaction can be summarised like this:

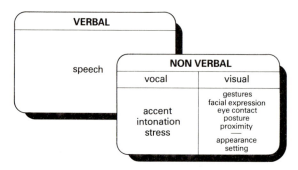

In language teaching we are, naturally, mainly concerned with the first, speech, along with its phonological accompaniments. With video we have the opportunity, if we want to take it, of paying attention to the visual as well. Let's consider the visual elements in more detail.

Gestures

These can be gestures we have learned and share with the rest of our own particular speech community, or they can be gestures which are purely idiosyncratic.

Learned gestures can often be restated in words. Examples in British society are:

— pointing to something = *there it is, sit there, that's the one I mean*
— nodding the head = *yes, I agree*

Idiosyncratic gestures, such as an individual's habit of tossing back a strand of hair, are more likely to be signals of personal character or state of mind which are transmitted unintentionally and unconsciously.

Facial expression

Like gesture, this may be consciously controlled or it may be something of which we are largely unaware. For example, you would probably associate raised eyebrows with the expression of surprise or disapproval and you might be conscious of raising your eyebrows to convey such an attitude. Did you know that human beings also raise their eyebrows when they greet each other as a signal of friendship to people they know? The 'eyebrow flash' as it has been called has been found to occur in many widely different cultures. Research has shown that we are normally not conscious that it takes place, but that we are uncomfortable if it is missing when we would expect it or present on inappropriate occasions — for example in a greeting from a complete stranger.

Eye contact

In some cultures eye contact between men and women is strictly forbidden outside the immediate family. In British culture this would make conversation very difficult as the extent and direction of gaze between people in a group plays a part in regulating their conversation and signalling who will speak next (turntaking). The direction and length of our gaze also conveys information about our attitudes to each other and to what is being said.

Posture

This is often called 'body language' and includes the way people stand or sit, the direction in which they turn their bodies, whether they lean forward or sit back. Elements of behaviour like these can function in a similar way to eye contact. We are all familiar with the tactic of turning one's back to keep a newcomer out of the group. Something similar to this can happen in discussion if a speaker does not want to let another interrupt. Studies of students taking part in seminars suggest that posture is also used to indicate a desire to enter the discussion.

Proximity

There are social norms within each culture as to the distance people stand or sit from each other. These differ from one culture to another and can consequently be misinterpreted and cause embarrassment or suspicion. The way people dispose themselves in the available space can also indicate, for example, their interpretation of the relative status of those present: for example, standing up when an important visitor enters the room.

Appearance

This includes features such as dress, hairstyles and personal belongings. They convey to someone who belongs to the same culture a lot of information about the person who is wearing or carrying them. Some of this kind of information is very culture-specific and in fact will sometimes have significance only to certain groups within a culture — think for example of 'old school ties'. Others become symbolic of a group or a nation — the bowler hat, the kilt. Many of these items are transient and date in much the same way as slang does, so that they then have connotations of certain historical periods as well.

Setting

We have expectations of how people will behave in certain physical surroundings: a church or a court of law imposes its own social norms. Again these will differ from one country to another and can change over the years. For viewers of video the location of a scene may provide many clues as to the content of an interaction, for example a shop. There are also many occasions when the two bear no apparent relation to each other. How much could you guess about a conversation between two people walking along a country lane for example?

The last two are different from the first five visual elements in that, although they also convey information, they are not part of the interaction in the same way. They are sometimes referred to as extralinguistic elements of communication.

Do we need to teach the visual elements of communication? There is no question that visual features are very much part of face-to-face communication. Now that we have video in the classroom the opportunity to focus on the visual is clearly there, so should we attempt to include it in a systematic way? Should we make sure that we work through a list of gestures, for example, in the same way that we cover a set of basic language functions in the beginners' syllabus?

One argument against teaching the visual is that, since it does not have to be translated by a non-native speaker in the way that language does, there is no need to make a systematic study of it. However people who are not familiar with the culture of a country do misinterpret situations and relationships and this can be due to a misunderstanding of visual clues. Visual clues in the main are clues to the social and cultural aspects of a message, whereas language carries the cognitive load.

The close association between the visual and the cultural may explain the reluctance of some teachers to give it much attention. In some countries and with some groups of learners English is learned purely as a vehicle to academic study or as a means of improving job prospects. It is seen as a necessary tool but it is not studied out of interest in the countries in which it is spoken. In such cases it is perfectly understandable that discussion of the culture from which a language grows is of minor importance and may in fact be actively discouraged.

In other situations the opposite is the case and there is considerable interest in placing the language in as broad a context as possible. Where this is the case, a study of visual communication would be very sensible. But how should it be done?

When we plan a language syllabus we can draw on very comprehensive descriptions of the language which provide us with a basis for deciding what should go into the syllabus and in what order. When it comes to a 'visual' syllabus, we don't know where to start. Visual communication has been categorised in various ways but none of them has succeeded in being comprehensive. Perhaps the most helpful classification for the language teacher is that of the American anthropologist Ray Birdwhistell who divides non-verbal signals into three types:

(a) Idiosyncratic

This includes personal 'tics', ways of moving one's head, habits such as nail-biting, which are peculiar to individuals and not generalisable to the whole group. We would not be likely to teach these in an ordered way any more than we would teach idiosyncratic features of individuals' speech patterns which are not typical of the speech community as a whole.

(b) Learned gesture

Some cultures make extensive use of learned gestures and they do indeed have to be learned in the same way as one learns the word for 'station' or how to refuse politely. Indeed for the refusal of food and drink there are a range of different visual signals: in different societies this may be signalled by putting a hand over a glass, by putting one's knife and fork in a particular way or by shaking one's head in a particular manner. The teaching of learned gesture could be approached in a systematic, comparative way, at least with monolingual groups, where differences between learned gesture in the students' own culture and in the target culture are often a subject of considerable interest.

(c) Continuous movement

Birdwhistell carried out some very detailed analysis of every movement made by people during a conversation. This and other studies revealed that shifts of posture, head movements and changing facial expression all have a part to play in the way a conversation moves from one person to another in a group. Our signals that we want to speak, or that we haven't yet finished speaking, are often sent visually and the signals are not the same in all cultures. While this is a complex area to tackle and it is by no means fully charted, it is worth looking at with some learners — for instance those who need to conduct business and to attend meetings in English.

In textbooks and audio material for language teaching the characters are usually there as pegs the language can be hung on. They don't have real relationships, they don't live in real places. The details are not filled in. This doesn't work with video, which is a literal medium demanding believable characters in believable situations. So there should be things to exploit in video material that we don't have to think about with other material we use in the classroom. Also with video we are quite likely to be using material which was not made for language teaching anyway and which will be full of visual elements we could exploit. How do we go about it?

It is not always easy to predict just what problems a particular group of learners is likely to have with any materials. This is perhaps even more the case with interpretations of visuals. It is therefore a good idea when preparing to teach a piece of video to start by viewing silently yourself on a first viewing before using a sequence in a lesson. Note your own interpretation of the sequence, then make a note of the interpretations you expect your students to make. Check it after the lesson to see how accurate your predictions were. This may help you identify visual elements which are unfamiliar to your students and would therefore make it easier to decide how much emphasis you should give to them and how you might introduce them. You can focus your students on visual elements by getting them to talk about a number of aspects of a scene.

Talking about the setting

Choose a sequence which opens with a general view of the setting. Many video programmes will include such shots — they're known as establishing shots. They are there to let the viewer get a feel for the location and the number of people in it before the camera goes in closer to cover the action. Use an establishing shot to check what your students have noticed and how they have interpreted it. Pause or stop the tape at the end of the shot and ask for suggestions about where it is. This could also be a place to introduce vocabulary your students will need in order to be able to follow the programme.

Talking about the characters

Choose a character who is central to the story, and pause as soon as this character appears on the screen. Ask students what they think his or her job is. What can they suggest about the character's background and personality? Ask them too what clues they are using. In this way you are getting the students involved in thinking about what they are looking at, and you are also getting an indication of how they interpret what they see. Do they understand the significance of a certain uniform for instance, or the kind of case a character is carrying?

Talking about the situation

Some drama excerpts would give rise to a lot of discussion about relationships between the characters. Choose a scene where much of this is conveyed visually and see how far everyone agrees in their interpretation of what they see. Ask about the roles of the characters — why are they there? This kind of discussion can throw up differences between cultures which we are often not aware of.

Silent viewing

We have already discussed in Chapter 4 the technique of silent viewing. A final point to make here is that another effect of silent viewing of video is the interest it generates and the way this manifests itself in commitment to a point of view about a scene. When viewing video, students at all levels attempt to make sense of what they see by hypothesising an event that suits a setting, or a setting that suits an event — it is not possible to say which comes first. Students can then get very involved in looking for clues to support their own hypotheses. As others may have different theories a genuine desire to prove a point of view leads to some lively debate. We all like solving problems and by focussing on the visual we can present a class with a range of problems to solve.

What about the verbal?

I've said a lot about the visual because that's what's new to us and it's also something that may be neglected. We are so accustomed to focussing on language, that there is a strong tendency in teaching with video to focus on the words in the same way we do with audio. If you treat a video sequence purely as a vehicle for language there are two dangers:

(a) You are overlooking visual clues which your students may be picking up. So you run the risk that they are thinking about one thing while you are pursuing another;
(b) You are keeping the focus on language and missing a good opportunity to focus on the message.

Of course we can teach video materials in a very similar way to audio materials. But we will make much better use of the medium if we seek to use it differently and for different reasons. Use it, for instance, to demonstrate to learners how much redundancy there is in normal spoken communication. Native speakers are accustomed to making a lot of assumptions from a few clues. They don't need to hear every syllable — if they hear most of the stressed syllables that will be enough. They also use a range of visual clues of the kind we spoke about earlier in this chapter. In addition they draw on all kinds of background information they may have about that particular situation. With well selected video material you could make this point by starting with a 'sound only' presentation, as Video Plan 4 in Chapter 4 does.

Using video at different learning levels

The experiences we organise for our learners vary according to the command of the language they have. This applies equally to the way we use video, which could be seen as having three distinct roles, depending on the learner level it is used at.

Basic level

With learners in the very early stages, the essence of all that we do is control. We control the amount and the complexity of language we expose them to. We limit the range of contexts to the most obvious ones. We organise activities which make very limited demands on the language control of the participants. We keep everything simple and repetitive.

Video's main role at this stage is to provide the learner with stepping stones to real world use of language by giving realistic examples of language in use in a limited range of contexts. The right kind of video material can transfer those limited bits of language to realistic situations outside the classroom and begin to bridge the gap between the two. If learners can see and recognise the language they've been studying in use in realistic situations this has two benefits:

(a) it validates the study they are doing by confirming that the language is used in the real world;
(b) it gives learners confidence in their ability to cope with the real situation.

For this we need material which provides as much visual support as possible and situations where the language is highly predictable.

Intermediate level

By the stage we define broadly as intermediate, learners are some way towards developing control of the language they are learning: their store of language has grown to a point where they can adapt, adjust and add to it with some facility; they can transfer language use from one context to another; they are building up more complex networks of language and the work we do in the classroom at this level is similarly more complex and less controlled.

Video's role now can be to provide the variety, interest and stimulation which are very important at this stage when motivation is often beginning to wane. This is the level at which the focus should begin to shift from isolated language items to the real use of those items to convey a message. Video is a good medium with which to move them away from the beginner's preoccupation with individual words to an attempt to follow the general drift of a message. Using video at this level is a good occasion to focus on the story or the way a topic is treated or the way a programme is structured. Encourage comment, speculation and prediction rather than asking for reproduction of what they have heard. Use a lesson based on video as an occasion to do something different.

Advanced level   By this stage learners are looking for opportunities to extend their already considerable store of language, to test their ability to retrieve from this store, to improve their fluency and to refine their control. At this level video can be the provider of real world experience if it is used to put advanced learners in the same position as native speakers. This is done by presenting them with programmes designed for native speakers and setting tasks which assume a high level of comprehension of the video material. The focus moves entirely onto the message within the programme and language becomes the tool which gives access to the message. Video can now be used mainly as a source of information and as a stimulus to classroom activity such as debate and discussion. Programmes can be viewed as programmes, and students encouraged to express their opinions as to how they were made and how effective they were. They can also be an input to a range of information-gathering activities.

7

Using a video camera in the classroom

To make a video recording in the classroom you need four things:

— a camera;
— a video recorder;
— a microphone;
— a cassette to record onto.

Recording equipment is becoming lighter, smaller, more portable and simpler to use and with most cameras nowadays you don't need to use extra lights, provided the room is reasonably bright. Chapter 2 goes into all the technical details. This chapter is about how and why you might make use of a camera as part of a language programme.

Recording student performance

In any kind of training a video camera offers the possibility of recording the trainees' performance. This in turn offers trainees the possibility of taking an objective look at their own performance and it gives trainers the chance to assess that performance.

This is particularly useful for people learning any kind of practical skill — how to assemble delicate instruments, how to apply bandages, how to serve at tennis. Video recording is also regularly used in training for situations where the ability to communicate is important. For example in preparing people for interviews or for public speaking. One trainee on a course for people looking for employment commented that seeing himself on video in a mock interview was an experience that changed his life. Seeing yourself as others see you won't be such a dramatic experience for everyone but it is certainly a compelling one and it can become an experience you learn from.

You can use a camera in the classroom to let learners see and hear themselves communicating in the target language. There are a number of activities you could record.

Talking to the
camera

*Camera position
to record one speaker*

Set your students the task of talking to the camera in the way a reporter or
newsreader does. They have to address an unseen audience through the
camera and they can prepare a script for their talk. But don't just treat this
as a language exercise. They can get so much more out of it if you
encourage them to approach it in the way a real production would be
approached — as an exercise in communicating something to a specific
audience.

An obvious and good choice of audience is their classmates because the
student 'reporters' will have a good idea of what would interest them. In
preparing the script, talk to them about writing for speaking. Scripts for
real broadcasts are written to be read aloud — sometimes to be read as
though they were spontaneous speech. Treating the task as a real one
introduces a real language exercise with the focus it puts on the difference
between written and spoken language.

Students can work individually or a group could prepare a set of 'mini
talks' about the same topic. Some ideas for topics are:

— reports on study projects;
— news items about the college or town;
— describe an object or a picture — viewers have to guess what it is —
  then show it;
— tell a story within a given length of time.

Interviews

*Camera position to
record an interview, where
only the interviewee
will be seen*

An interview elicits spontaneous speech in a way a prepared talk does not.
Students can be interviewed by each other, by their teacher, or by someone

brought in for the purpose. The camera work can be kept as simple as it is for recording one person giving a talk — it can stay on the interviewee. It's sufficient simply to hear the questions the interviewer puts. The person to be interviewed should be given some indication of the topic and possibly of the kinds of questions they might be asked but it is important that there should not be any rehearsal of the interview as they will then lose their spontaneity. The purpose of recording interviews is to give students a chance to see themselves in a situation where they can't predict the direction an exchange may take. So they have to use whatever language they have at their disposal. For students taking examinations which feature interviews, this exercise would be particularly useful. If you can record interviews at different points in a course, then edit the same student's interviews onto one tape, you provide an encouraging record for the student of the progress she or he is making.

Acting out a situation

Many of us ask our students to act at some points in our lessons. The purpose of this is usually to allow students the opportunity to use language they know in a less controlled situation. This acting can range from pairs of students re-enacting a dialogue through to a simulation involving the whole class. In recording this kind of activity you are recording student 'performance' in two senses — performance of a communicative act in the target language and performance of a role. It is important to remember this when it comes to playback and this is discussed in the next section.

The making of a video recording provides a goal for learners to work towards and this is a motivating factor. If they know the performance is to be recorded, their practice of a roleplay situation has a real purpose and their performance is likely to have a sharper edge to it. The fact that they are performing to a camera instead of just for the teacher or the rest of the class makes the whole thing less artificial. We *do* put on a performance for the camera, whereas we don't usually 'perform' our everyday conversations to an audience.

All the activities suggested for video recording are activities with a language learning purpose which could of course be done without the presence of the camera. They often are. Students present to the rest of the class, or just to the teacher. Why then bother to video record it? If you have access to a camera this is a question you should think about carefully. It's easy to become enthusiastic about ideas for using something new, without stopping to think through your reasons for doing it.

We have looked at two reasons you might have for recording student performance:

— to analyse that performance;
— to provide motivation for the task set.

These are reasons for recording rather than simply performing to the class but wouldn't audio recording do just as well?

The answer to that question is that it depends how you plan to use the recording. If it is to be worked on by one person for detailed analysis of the language produced — perhaps for research purposes, or to help a teacher note common language problems — then audio alone would be sufficient. If it is intended for anything other than intensive individual study, then, if you've got a camera, video is easier to 'listen' to. Also if the focus is on an ability to communicate then it is better to be able to see the visual as well as the aural aspects of the interaction. A final technical point on audio versus video recording: it takes no longer to set up for a simple video recording than it does to position a microphone for an audio recording.

Playback sessions

We must assume that *someone* wants to see a recording, otherwise there was no point in recording it in the first place. But does the whole class want to see it? Most of us want to see ourselves on the screen — although it may turn out to be an unpleasant experience! — but we're not usually terribly interested in watching the performance of others. So before you automatically play back the recordings to the class, ask yourself these questions:

— Does the whole class need to see it?
— What do you expect them to gain from it?
— Can you justify the time needed to view, say, the recordings of five groups, which may run for five minutes each — a total of twenty-five minutes?

You may decide that a recording only needs to be viewed by the people involved in making it. If, for example, you have had the class working in groups to prepare a programme for video recording, you should try to organise things so that both recording and playback sessions can be done in rotation. This requirement is no different from any other kind of groupwork which allows for variation in pace of working and provides alternative tasks for those who finish first. The additional organisational problem is to have the video equipment you need set up so that recording and playback sessions don't disrupt the working of the other groups.

The most convenient arrangement is to have separate viewing and recording rooms so that the two activities can go on simultaneously and groups preparing to record, or working on other tasks, can work undistracted. However, as most places don't have such luxurious room provision you could look into the possibility of screening corners of the room in some way.

Another problem may be that you only have one machine for both recording and playback so that only one of these activities can go on at one time. In this case you could organise recording sessions on one day, with playback sessions the next, both done as rotating group tasks. You can also of course be selective about both activities. It is not necessary to record and playback each group each time.

Reasons for having playback sessions

When a recording of a student performance is done mainly for motivational purposes, the language learning objectives are achieved through the performance of the task itself. A viewing of the end result is not strictly necessary if the main point of the exercise was to have students perform a task which required them to communicate with each other in English as they did it. However from the students' point of view, the making of a video recording was the purpose of the exercise. If it is not viewed the motivation will not be there next time round.

If the recording was made so that student performance could be assessed then obviously playback is essential. Whether it is done in groups, with individuals or with the whole class, everyone viewing should be involved in a positive way in carrying out the evaluation. This means that they should be clear about what they are to look for in the performance and how they are to judge these points.

Viewing tasks

Let's take the recording task described earlier: to prepare news items for a magazine programme or news broadcast. What judgements could the audience be asked to pass when it is played back?

They could focus on performance:

— did the 'newsreader' appear confident and convincing?
— was the presentation clear and easy to follow?

They could focus on language production:

— were there any errors of grammar or vocabulary?
— was stressing, pausing and intonation good?

They could focus on content:

— were the news items interesting?
— were they believable?

Viewing by the whole class

Playback to the whole class may be unavoidable because of time and space restrictions. In this case the original recording task can take account of this and capitalise on it. If as part of the task you specify the effect the programme is to have on the audience, you are building in the criteria by which that audience can judge the programme and you are giving them a purpose in viewing. For example the task could be to produce a news item which would amuse the audience, or which would surprise the audience, or which would make them very happy. Each member of the audience would then have the task in the playback group of giving each item points, say on a scale from one to five, according to how well it achieved its aim. The playback session now has a purpose for everyone and, incidentally, a lot of listening and discussion is going on.

The individual performers will be interested in other factors too as will the teacher, and they can have their own checklist of language performance points to look for. But for whole class playback sessions the general focus should be on things which affect everyone in the group.

The teacher's role in playback sessions

Our automatic reaction as teachers is to correct language errors when we hear them. It's better to control that reaction in a playback session where the focus is on other aspects of learner performance. You can note problems for later. Remember that you have asked students to put on a public performance. Show your appreciation of it. Try to find some aspect that you can praise genuinely. Some learners find it an ordeal to appear

79

before a camera. Some find a playback session even more of an ordeal. You will have your own way of dealing with these reactions but one of the teacher's functions in a group playback session is to be aware of individual reactions of this kind and to steer discussion away from subjective comment if necessary.

Giving students the camera

So far we have discussed uses of the camera which are organised by the teacher. In some language schools it is possible to give the camera a different function: it is handed over to student groups to be used as a tool in project work. A group of students undertakes as a project to produce a video programme. They do the whole thing themselves: deciding content, researching, planning the programme, writing scripts, acting, making costumes, operating the camera. This is excellent groupwork as there are so many different jobs to do and different talents can therefore be accommodated.

This kind of access to recording facilities is not of course practicable in many language teaching situations but it has considerable potential on intensive courses where students have many contact hours. In that situation variety of activity is needed and it is also often possible to allocate times when students can choose between several options. In a close-knit community of students the video camera is sometimes used for a video club which produces a video magazine about the affairs of the college. Video Plan 18 is an example of a recording task set for a group of university students. Note how the organisation of the task is suggested in various ways, particularly through the schedule that is given.

VIDEO PLAN 18: A video recording project

(From *An Intensive Theme-Oriented Course in Advanced English for First-Semester German University Students of Diverse Subject Studies*)

University Architecture

Today you are going to make a film based on your impressions of a particular area of this building. Once you know which area you will be dealing with, it will be your task to produce a film about it. This film should be similar to the type of film we have seen already — with a commentator, interviewer and interviewees.

In thinking about the part of the building where you will do the filming, please consider its aesthetic, practical and social aspects. Discuss (a) what its present appearance and use are, (b) whether or not this is the way it should be and (c) what feasible improvements you could recommend for it.

Please keep to the following times:

9.15-9.45:	fact-finding
	impression-gathering
9.45-10.45:	organisation
	script-writing
	rehearsals of interviews and commentary
11.00-12.15:	filming

The purpose of student production

Where it is feasible to let students take it over, the camera is simply a tool used to carry out a task which students find engrossing, exciting and therefore highly motivating. When the group is multilingual and all communication has to be in the target language, an absorbing task of this kind is an excellent communicative activity. When the group is monolingual there is a real problem that because the task is so interesting, the use of English is forgotten in the urgency of the moment. It is possible to specify that a production should not be a silent movie and the end result is therefore in English. Some teachers consider this sufficient to justify the time spent, others don't. It all depends on how you interpret the objectives of your language programme.

8

Using video playback in teacher training

This chapter looks at the roles video can have in teacher training and at materials associated with these roles. It also considers problems that may arise in using video with teacher trainees.

Video material that could be used in teacher training can be grouped in a similar way to material for teaching:

— there is published material specifically designed for use in the training of teachers to teach English as a Second or Foreign Language. (See Appendix 1: Teacher Training Materials.)

— it is also possible to draw on materials not designed for this purpose;

— institutions with video cameras and editing equipment can build up a collection of their own materials.

Any of these types of material can be used with groups as part of a formal training session or, if self-access viewing facilities exist, they could form the basis of individual study tasks.

Roles for video in teacher training

The big advantage of film or video in teacher training is that it gives trainees access to a range of classrooms they could not otherwise enter.

Most teacher-training programmes include provision for trainees to sit in with other teachers so that they get some experience of the environment they will work in. First-hand experience is invaluable but only a limited amount of it can be arranged and you certainly can't have large numbers of trainees sitting at the back of the same class. With examples of teaching on video any number of observers can share and discuss the same experience. Video also creates the opportunity to observe a wider range of teacher personalities, teaching styles, classroom conditions and learning needs. Observation materials can be of two kinds.

Demonstration
material

Some teacher-training material is designed to show teachers how teaching should be done. Implicitly or explicitly it aims to provide a model of some kind. Early teacher training series like the BBC's *View and Teach* feature lessons which have been planned and filmed in order to illustrate specific points. The programmes consist of excerpts from recorded classes which are then discussed during the programme. The British Council's five films from their English Language Teaching Institute are also of this kind, each one featuring innovative techniques in a different area of classroom practice. *Communication Games in a Language Programme* is an example. Another BBC series, *Teaching Observed*, groups examples from classrooms in different parts of the world under themes like teaching reading and ESP teaching. Each of these series uses commentary to explain and underline the main points and some include comment from the teachers seen in the film.

There are video programmes designed to introduce new methods, such as the Silent Way method, which combine an explanation of the approach with examples of groups being taught. Publishers launching new materials sometimes produce demonstration tapes showing the materials being taught. This is a good way of letting people judge for themselves how they work. The value of demonstration can extend to subjects like testing. Some institutions have used video to record good and bad ways of conducting oral tests, for example.

Demonstration materials are clearly designed from the beginning to put over a specific message. That message is spelt out within the programme through commentary and interviews and the examples shown have often been specially set up to illustrate it.

Case study material

In contrast, case study materials aim to capture a real lesson as it happens in normal classroom conditions (although it is never entirely normal to have a camera pointing at you while you go about your daily business.) Viewers are left to draw their own conclusions from what they see and there is no overt commentary built into the programme. Of course there is implicit commentary in any selection of examples but case study material is intended to be seen as a working document which is left open to varied and flexible use in a teacher-training programme.

Much teacher-training material currently being produced tends to be of this kind. The Inner London Education Authority (ILEA) records in schools throughout its area for this purpose; the BBC's Open University Production Centre has recently produced a series for the training of adult education tutors following this approach; the British Council is experimenting with edited lessons which are accompanied by an extensive index to help trainers put together their own selection of classroom examples. In addition, these last materials include four programmes which have been put together around common themes in teacher-training, such as classroom management. In these the selection has been done for the trainer.

The end result may sometimes be less polished than purpose-made demonstration material but case study material is intended as a working document of current classroom practice and it has the advantage of flexibility in the ways it can be used.

Using video in teacher training sessions

All that we said in Part 2 about exploiting the control video gives us over the material is as relevant to the teacher trainer as it is to the teacher. The problem of passive viewing is also just as real and viewing tasks are just as important. The approach is similar: select sequences of the right length for your purpose; set previewing tasks or questions; allow time for follow-up discussion.

Preparation for viewing could include a reading assignment to be completed before the viewing session. Group discussion of a topic could precede a viewing. For the viewing stage give teachers a checklist of things to look for, or questions to be answered after viewing.

Film of the real thing is an excellent way of challenging misconceptions or assumptions people make about a situation and a good aim for viewing tasks is to make trainees sharper in their perception of what is happening around them. It is quite common in talking about teaching to focus on what the teacher does and to forget the effect this may have on the learner. Viewing tasks can usefully lead the viewer to concentrate on the learner for a change by setting observation tasks focussed on learner behaviour and learner reactions. Video Plan 19 gives two examples of viewing tasks for observation materials.

VIDEO PLAN 19: Viewing tasks for teacher trainees

(From *Teaching and Learning in Focus*)

DESCRIPTION	SUGGESTIONS FOR EXPLOITATION
INDICATING THAT A MISTAKE HAS BEEN MADE Ten very short sequences showing different teachers responding to error.	**Anticipation** 1. How can a teacher indicate to a learner that he has made a mistake without actually correcting him? Make a list. 2. What are the important things to bear in mind here? Why might a teacher have to be a bit careful? **Observation** How do these teachers react when a mistake is made? Note down any techniques not anticipated in your discussion. **Discussion** What do you feel about the techniques you have just seen? Are some more effective than others? Are some more complicated? Are some less tactful? Which do/would you use? Which don't/wouldn't you? Why?
LEARNERS SPONTANEOUSLY HELPING ONE ANOTHER Two sequences illustrating how learners help and correct each other without bidding. The first sequence shows learners during a whole class activity controlled by the teacher. The second shows complete beginners working in pairs on their very first roleplay. (Only part of the unit is reproduced here)	**Observation** What do these two sequences illustrate? **Discussion** Why does one learner help or correct another? How does the person who is helped feel? Compare the two sequences in response to these questions.

Problems

There are such obvious advantages in having access through video to examples of teaching that it is easy to forget that there can also be problems. When teachers look at examples of other teachers in action, there are some fairly common reactions:

(a) It's a great opportunity to pick holes in the way the class is conducted. There's always something that could have gone better in any lesson — and there will always be at least two views as to how it should have been conducted anyway. Any group viewing a classroom recording is likely to notice a variety of different things. And they will disagree about their relative importance. They may pick on a teacher's mannerisms, dress, or accent and discussion of something like this can dominate a session. This is where you need to establish a focus before viewing through the task you set. Another strategy is to make deliberate allowance for subjective reactions with an initial viewing task which simply lets trainees loose with their opinions. Then return to the material to analyse it from other points of view.

(b) Trainees can't make a connection between what they see and their own teaching environment. This is often a problem. Examples of teaching practice are rejected because they seem too remote from the trainees' own situation: 'Yes but ... my students would never (work in pairs/bring things to class/respond to a video screen.)' The classrooms shown on the video may be better resourced, classes may be smaller, the learners' backgrounds may be very different from those your trainees will meet. If this is the case, you need to think about how you can make it clear to your trainees what the purpose of the viewing is. Again perhaps an initial discussion which does focus on the differences to get that out of the way might be helpful. Then set a task which requires trainees to apply what they have seen to their own situation.

(c) It is rejected because it is decontextualised. Film of classes is inevitably selective. It is usually heavily edited and in any case a camera does not 'look' at a scene in the same way that the human eye does. A common reaction from viewers of filmed classes is that they can't assess what they see because they don't have enough information about the class. They can't put the extract in its context and this too can lead them to reject what they are shown. This is difficult to deal with and producers of teacher-training materials have tackled the problem in different ways. In documentary-style demonstration material the commentary is used to provide background information. With case study material print has an important role but there is always the danger that it goes astray or just doesn't get read. Captions on the screen can give brief information about what went on in the missing bits and how much time has elapsed. It is helpful if trainers have as much information as possible so that they can set the context for trainees at the time of the viewing.

Using other kinds of material

Another possible use of video in a training programme is to trigger new ideas and expand trainees' horizons. This doesn't require material made specifically for teacher training. We can exploit video's power to present vividly situations which are unfamiliar or inaccessible to us. Teachers of multi-ethnic classes need to develop some awareness of the backgrounds of their students. In other contexts, trainees who are going to teach a language not their own may need to extend their experience of the culture of that language. This element of a training programme can be based round all manner of video materials which present aspects of that culture.

All kinds of video material could provide a lead into discussion of the psychological and social aspects of teaching. Anything which features social interaction could lead on to group discussion of some aspect of communication. For example it could be used to get a group to make a list of all the means of communication they noticed, as a starting point for a session on one particular aspect of communication.

It is worth checking what is available on video with a view to picking short sequences which could be used as mind stretchers occasionally at the beginning of a training session.

Using recorded lectures

One in-house use of cameras popular with many institutions is the recording of visiting 'gurus'. On the face of it this seems like a good idea. It's reasonably straightforward as a recording task (discussed in the next chapter) and it gives an ephemeral occasion a longer lease of life. Those who miss the lecture can see it later and those who attend the course in years to come can at least have the video lecture even if they can't have the real thing. It's certainly worth a try but reactions of the viewing audience should be carefully monitored.

The experience of watching someone lecture to a live audience is very different from being there yourself. It's also very different from watching live teaching although superficially the situations seem similar. The difference lies in your purpose in watching the two. A group of teachers in training watch a recording of a class as a piece of data to be analysed. They are benefitting from the opportunity to eavesdrop on an interaction. Their expectations of a lecture aimed at an audience similar to themselves will be very different. A lecture is aimed directly at its audience. Factors like eye contact between lecturer and individuals in the audience give members of the audience an impression, however slight, that they are in communication with the lecturer. The lecturer responds to feedback from the audience — conveyed by smiles and nods, body position and posture, laughter, silence or, in extreme cases, departure from the room. All of this immediacy is missing from the experience of viewing the same lecture recorded on video. As a result the viewing audience may feel alienated and become bored or hostile unless the original lecture is interesting enough to overcome this reaction.

If there are good arguments for using video regularly as a carrier of lectures — sometimes the case in a programme which is repeated in several centres — then there may be equally good arguments for planning and recording them as video programmes. Production of this kind is described in the next chapter.

Organising self-access use of teacher training video material

Where it is possible to arrange viewing facilities, a bank of classroom recordings for teachers to refer to in their own time is a sensible and useful resource. However, if it is to be well used, it needs to be well organised. For a start, make it as easy as possible for teachers to have access to the resource. Check that machines and materials will be available at times that suit them. Consider a loan system if teachers have video machines at home. Then make sure that they know what is there, how they can use it and why they should use it. If trainees are attending a regular in-service training course, individual viewing could be built into the syllabus. This obviously saves time in group sessions, but only if everyone does it.

Now check the materials you are suggesting trainees look at. If a self-access library is to be effective, you need to spend time viewing every recording, putting yourself in the position of trainees sitting down on their own to make what they can of it. If they are looking at video recordings of classes, trainees will need some guidance in their viewing. All the suggestions we have made for previewing and viewing activities apply to this situation even more strongly. Every classroom recording in a self-access video library for trainees should have a worksheet to go with it. This also applies to recorded lectures — particularly if they show handouts being used. Provide what support you can in the way of information about the event and guidance about what to look for in it.

Finally it is a good idea to devise a way of checking what use is made of a self-access video service. The system may look very good in theory, but does anyone actually come in and look at the tapes? This question is particularly important for institutions which are investing time in making their own video recordings. If it turns out that very few trainees are making use of the service, try to find out why this is. There may be a practical problem of access, which could perhaps be sorted out. On the other hand, if the recordings are not proving useful, then perhaps you should think again about making them.

9

Using a camera in teacher training

The most common — and probably the most sensible — reason institutions give for getting a video camera is for teacher training. This chapter looks at the uses they may put it to.

Recording teachers as part of their training

Video cameras have an important role in training for any profession which works with people. For example, they are often used with people who have to conduct interviews. The video camera's objective eye records an activity where several things happen at once: the interviewer is talking, responding, assessing, deciding which topic to introduce next; the interviewee is interpreting, responding, reacting to the situation and so on. It is not easy for an observer to notice everything that is going on. It is impossible for the participants to distance themselves from the situation sufficiently to analyse their own behaviour in all its complex detail. Playback of the recording, as often as necessary, provides the occasion for objective judgement. Classroom interaction is even more complex than an interview because of the size of the group and the choices the teacher constantly makes about how to respond to what learners say.

Letting trainees see themselves teach may seem in itself a good enough reason for recording teachers teaching: the benefits of being able to see themselves as their students see them appear to be so obvious. But if the purpose is no more precisely formulated than that, the playback session may never get beyond teachers' purely subjective reactions to seeing themselves on the screen.

Recording teachers teaching in order to play it back to them is sometimes loosely described as microteaching. By itself this is not microteaching but the same principles can be applied even if a full programme is not being followed. A microteaching programme is based on an analysis of the skills a teacher employs in the classroom. Trainees are focussed on one skill at a time, in a step by step programme. They teach small groups of students very short lessons concentrating on one particular set of skills. The lessons are recorded so that the trainee's performance can be reviewed and measured against criteria which have been set down for that skill. Following the review stage they may then repeat the cycle of preparation — teaching — feedback all over again in an attempt to improve their performance of that skill. The recording need not be a video recording but video is perhaps the most effective means of providing a basis for feedback sessions.

Even though it may not be possible or desirable to run a full-scale programme of this kind, it is sensible to agree the purpose of making a video recording and, from that, criteria to apply to the end result. Teachers are more likely to learn something from a recording if they have specific points to look for. Here are some examples:

(a) The setting up of roleplay
— Do learners know what they are expected to do?
— How long did it take to explain?
— Are the objectives of the exercise clear?
— How long do they spend on it?
— Does everyone participate as they should?

(b) Correcting learners
— What kinds of error does the teacher correct?
— Is there a rationale to this?
— Was each correction necessary at that point?
— Did it seem to help the learner?

(c) Use of aids
— If an aid is used, why is it used?
— What does it contribute?
— Is it well prepared?
— Is the teacher confident about using it?

(d) Groupwork
— What happens when students work in groups?
— Do they do what is expected of them?
— Do they revert to their native tongue?
— Do they seem to understand what they are doing?
— What is the purpose of the groupwork?

If regular recording is possible, teachers could be trained to monitor themselves using a checklist of this kind. Individuals could have their own list of points to consider. It is not as highly structured a programme as microteaching would demand but it applies some microteaching principles in the emphasis placed on the elements of classroom interaction.

Organising classroom recording

A camera always looks at a scene from a particular point of view. In a classroom it can give you the students' view of the teacher, it can give you the teacher's view of the students or it can be an observer which sits at the side of the class and looks from one to the other.

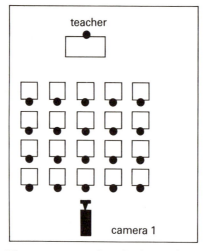

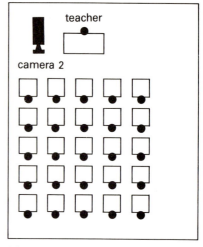

The camera records only the teacher   *The camera records only the students*

A lot of discussion about teaching centres on the teacher and the teacher's role as performer, manager or lecturer. Trainee teachers are quite naturally concerned with their own performance and much of their training has to focus on what they do in the classroom. The goal of their training must however be to make them aware of their learners. A video camera offers a powerful way to do this. Try a recording in which the camera looks at the class the whole time so that it gives you the teacher's-eye view. If a lesson involves groupwork, you might even experiment with keeping the camera fixed on one group of learners — it is possible to lock it off without an operator and it need not be too obvious to students that they are being singled out. Set the microphone so that it picks up that group and use the resulting recording to set tasks for trainees which focus them on the learner.

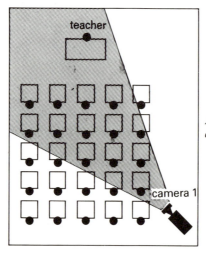

A fixed camera with a wide-angle lens

The questions given above under 'Groupwork' are intended to encourage trainees to look for evidence as to the effectiveness of the technique and the teacher's use of it.

Some institutions have experimented with a fixed camera operated by the teacher, so that no one else needs to be in the room to operate the camera. A camera with a wide-angle lens is fixed high up on the wall at a point where it takes in the widest angle of the room. It is linked to a video recorder in the room and all the teacher has to do is to switch on when she or he wants to be recorded.

This has its limitations as it only records what happens in one part of the room and there is no possibility of changing the angle or going in closer to one group. However for immediate playback to the teacher concerned these limitations may be acceptable. It will depend on how clearly the teacher perceives the purpose of making the recording.

Playback

Classes are fine when you're teaching them or learning in them, very long and boring when you're just an observer. The same problems can arise at playback sessions as with recordings of student performance. You need to think about who will be involved in the playback session and what should be recorded. It is not necessary to record a whole class each time. You could decide in advance to record one activity, or to record only one particular stage of the lesson. It is useful to draw up with the teacher concerned a list of points to concentrate on, both during the recording and at the subsequent playback.

There is no need for the whole group to watch playback sessions — it is a much better use of time to train teachers to monitor themselves and to consult their tutor when they feel the need for it. This requires some time to be spent on organising access to playback machines and on introducing teachers to the concept, but that time is well spent as it then frees the tutor to give individual guidance to teachers with problems.

Wider uses of classroom recording

So far we have looked at recording a teacher as a part of that teacher's own training. The suggestion has been that only the teacher concerned need see the results, probably along with a tutor. Generally recordings of this kind have a very short and limited shelf life. The next lesson is recorded over the one before — and teachers should always have the security of knowing that a recording will be erased if they request it.

In addition to this kind of recording there may be a good case for producing your own teacher training materials, based on in-house recording. This could be useful for two reasons:

— to fill gaps in published teacher-training materials;
— to demonstrate materials and methods in use in a local context.

The last reason is a powerful one and could be a solution to the problem of trainees rejecting examples of teaching practice because it is too remote from their own situation. Tapes of local examples can be put together quite simply, by editing together selections from appropriate recordings. But they do have to be selected — and that takes a lot of viewing time — and they do have to be edited — and that requires more time and some editing skills. (See Chapter 1 on editing.) Going into a training session with a pile of separate cassettes and having to find the bit you want on each one is for emergencies only. It is an unprofessional, time-consuming and inefficient way to use video recordings.

It is best to plan in advance what kind of demonstration tape you want and then you have the possibility of recording for that purpose. In this way examples can be collected in a methodical way and edited with the minimum expenditure of time on viewing and selecting extracts from long recordings.

Recording lectures

The use of recordings of visiting speakers was discussed in the last chapter. If there is a need for it, there are two ways of approaching this type of production.

Recording lectures as they happen

This assignment is very similar to recording classes. Camera positions will be much the same, except that there is probably more interest in seeing the lecturer and less in the audience than is the case with teacher and class. You should however show something of the audience, particularly in the early stages of the lecture, otherwise someone viewing the recording has no idea who the speaker is talking to. You must get the lecturer's permission to record and use the recording and it's a good idea too to find out in advance what aids will be used. If the speaker is going to refer to headings on a blackboard, or diagrams on an Overhead Projector you have to make sure that the viewer too can refer to them. It may often be advisable to have essential reference material produced in print to accompany the recording, and you should certainly do this with any handouts the speaker distributes. If there is a break in recording during the lecture for any reason, you will also have to find a way of telling the viewer what happened in the gap.

Producing a video lecture

Looking at a lecture on video is not the same as being present at it. We suggested in the last chapter that in some situations you might think about producing a lecture on video instead of recording it as it happens. Plan the whole thing as a video production, working through the stages outlined in Chapter 11. Forget the original lecture situation and sit down with the speaker to work out the best way of communicating his or her message on the video screen. You can have the speaker in close-up, talking directly to the camera. You can put words, drawings and pictures on the screen. You can aim the whole thing directly at your viewing audience.

This type of recording requires considerably more sophistication in equipment, operation of the equipment and, above all, in the production skills of planning to meet educational objectives through an effective use of the medium.

It is very easy to start with plans for a simple recording and to end up trying to do something much more complex. If appropriate production skills and resources are not available, the end result doesn't usually reflect the time, thought and enthusiasm that went into it. The final chapter outlines what is involved in production planning if a video recording is to have any lasting impact.

10

Learner access to video playback

Learner access to video playback outside the classroom is becoming increasingly possible at a time when 'self-access' or 'individualised learning' is receiving a lot of attention from the teaching profession. It is an attractive concept: learners work at their own pace and make their own choices about what and how they will study. However learning by yourself is not easy. If the students we teach have access to video, we need to help them use this opportunity to develop their control of the language they are studying.

They may have access to video outside the classroom in their own homes or perhaps there is some arrangement in the language school which allows them to use the video player when it isn't in use in the classroom. You may be in an institution which has video-viewing facilities in the library and a selection of English language programmes for learners to borrow. If this is the case, check what materials there are — you might be able to make suggestions to your students about programmes they would find interesting to watch. Encourage them to take every opportunity they find to listen to the language. The more they are exposed to it, the more they are likely to acquire.

Helping the lone viewer

Students working alone with a video player are in the same position as a teacher using the machine in the classroom — they are in control of the machine and can exploit that fact in similar ways. Your students may have seen you play a sequence without sound then rewind for a second viewing, or pause to speculate about what might happen next. It may not have occurred to them that they could do the same when viewing video by themselves. Of course the situation is not the same and the techniques you use with a five-minute sequence in the classroom obviously wouldn't work with a sixty-minute film. But it might help your learners if they used some of your techniques for the first five or ten minutes of viewing. Talk to them about it and make sure that they understand the purpose of techniques like silent viewing and prediction. Encourage them to be active viewers. Below are some guidelines you could give them for using video on their own.

1. Find out what materials you have access to:
— Can you record English language broadcasts?
— Can you hire or borrow English language video programmes?
— Are there any special facilities available? (For example, in Britain it is now possible with the right kind of TV set to call up a whole range of information onto the TV screen. This includes the provision of English subtitles for some popular programmes. This service is intended for people who are hard of hearing but it could also help language learners follow the programme.)

2. Find out what you can do with the machine:
— Can you stop and start it when you want to?
— Can you turn the sound off?
— Do you know how to use the zero counter?
You can use the control you have to help you get more benefit from your viewing.

3. Think before you view:
— Before you switch on, spend a few minutes thinking about what you expect the programme to be about. Does the title give you any clues? Have you heard anything about the programme? Make notes of your ideas about the content of the programme. It helps to have something to listen for — such as checking whether your predictions were correct.

4. Don't let the programme run away with you:
— Pause frequently to ask yourself what the programme is about. Are you following the main thread of the argument, or the basics of the plot? Do you know who the characters are? Are you clear about the topic that is under discussion?
— If you can't answer these kinds of question, rewind and look at the section again. Then try to predict what will come next.
— Continue pausing in this way until you feel completely confident that you can follow the main points of the programme.

Providing
worksheets

In addition to giving guidelines for individual viewing, in some circumstances it might be worth producing worksheets for some of the programmes in the library stock. Obviously this would only apply to programmes which would be used by many language learners.

The tasks you set should be designed to help meet the individual learner's main purpose in viewing, so you need to define that purpose. A general purpose for leisure viewing would be to give the learner the experience of getting information and enjoyment from viewing a programme which was made for native speakers. This should be a rewarding and therefore a motivating experience if the learner does come away from it with a feeling of achievement.

How can a worksheet help this to happen? It should guide the learner to concentrate on the main points and help him/her follow the argument or the plot step by step. It could treat the programme in sections and set tasks that help the learner identify the main points made in each section. This could be done through questions, by building up a diagram of some kind, by giving a synopsis with gaps in it, or simply by giving a résumé in the learner's native language. The techniques will depend on the materials, the kind of learners you have and the kinds of task they are accustomed to doing. Don't devise questions just for the sake of having something on a worksheet. Concentrate on the main points of the programme.

The importance of
collecting feedback

Remember that the point about self-access is that the learners make their own choices about how they will use the resources at their disposal. You can only suggest ways they might go about it and provide what help you think they might need. They may choose to ignore this entirely. If you do aim to encourage them to use viewing facilities and if you produce any guidelines or worksheet support, try to find unobtrusive ways of checking whether they are used.

Self-access to video for language learners is something we haven't thought about much up to now and these suggestions are experimental. However the way technology is developing suggests that it is an area we should pay more and more attention to.

**Organising group
viewings**

Some teachers organise evening 'filmshows' using the school's video machine. In places where there is little opportunity to see films in English this sounds like a very good idea. It gives students access to another source of spoken English and it gives them one or two hours' exposure to the language. Most importantly they come to see a film, not to a language class, so the language is a means to an end. However an audience of learners is not the same as the audience of native speakers for whom the film was made and the experience of some teachers has been disappointing. There is a steady shuffle of people leaving once the film has started as they find it is so difficult to follow that the experience is frustrating. The end result is that learners feel very discouraged because it makes them feel that they know less than they thought. Here are some suggestions for tackling this problem.

Break the viewing up into chunks

This is not as heretical a suggestion as it might seem at first sight. After all most of us are accustomed with commercial television to having our viewing interrupted for advertisement breaks. So why not have 'comprehension breaks' for an audience of language learners? How you organise the breaks will depend on your audience. You could give them two minutes to check with their neighbours what they think has happened. You could provide a quick summary yourself, or, if you have time to do it, you could provide a written summary broken into sections corresponding to the points at which you have the breaks.

The purpose of these breaks is to give learners a chance to catch up with the plot; to get them to a point where they understand enough of what has happened to make a reasonable stab at following the gist of the next part.

Get films with subtitles

In a monolingual situation, films with subtitles in the national language may be available on video. This too is a good way of providing learners with extended exposure to the target language with the support of the subtitles to help them keep pace with the plot. It is usually possible to read subtitles in less time than it takes the characters to complete the exchange. So the viewer can find out what will be said and then listen to how it is said.

Choose your films carefully

Look for films with which your learners will be familiar in some way. For example, a dubbed version of a popular film may be showing locally. Or you may be able to get the film of a book they know. Look for anything that gives them a better chance of following the plot.

Interactive video

We saw in Chapter 1 that it is possible to link videocassette and videodisc machines to computers. The combination with videodisc players is particularly interesting because of the ways random access can be exploited. The use of computer-driven video has attracted the title 'Interactive Video'. The interactivity lies in the computer's capacity to respond to what the user does. Linked to video materials, this opens up all kinds of possibilities for learning by individuals or small groups.

Currently there are three possible levels of interactive use, determined by the properties of the different systems:

(a) Basic interactive features offered by the videodisc machine

Remote control and rapid random access are the key features which allow you to use a keypad or other remote control device to move through a video programme by your chosen route. These combine with forward and reverse in fast or slow motion, freeze and step frame (the ability to move one frame at a time) and two audio tracks. The interactive element is built into the programme in the form of 'menus'. These are lists of choices you are offered at certain points. This lets you decide what you want to see next. The table on page 97 shows how this can be used.

A PROGRAMME OFFERING FIVE STORIES
WITH 'MENUS' OF CHOICES FOR THE VIEWER

First choice, offered when the programme is started:

CHOOSE YOUR STORY

A: Story 1   D: Story 4

B: Story 2   E: Story 5

C: Story 3

Second choice, offered at the beginning of each story:

A: TEST YOUR VOCABULARY FIRST

This might include a sequence of still frames of vocabulary which features in the story and which can be illustrated. It could start by showing the pictures for the viewer to label, then, when the viewer chooses, a repeat with captions can be called up.

A further list of words which cannot be visualised could also appear. When ready, the viewer can choose to see a translation or dictionary definition.

B: VIEW WITH ENGLISH SUBTITLES

Goes straight into the story with subtitles.

C: ASSISTED VIEWING

This would take the viewer through the story in the way a teacher might do in the classroom.

The story is treated in sections. There are preview questions and viewing tasks for each section.

Answers and further instructions are given at the end of each task/section.

D: STRAIGHT VIEWING

Goes straight into the story.

Final choice, offered at the end of each story:

TEST YOURSELF

Questions to test comprehension of that story.

At any point the viewer can choose to come back to this 'menu' of choices and choose to take a different option.

(b) A video player with a built-in computer

Videodisc systems can have a small computer built into the video player. This adds two features: the capacity to branch in different directions and

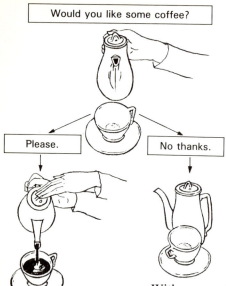

the capacity to keep a record of what the user does. A computer program can be encoded on the disc's surface and then loaded into the microprocessor in the videodisc player. This is not possible with videocassette players.

Branching makes it possible, for example, to program for different responses. This means that the user is not just offered a menu of choices but can also be asked questions. The program is written so that the answer 'yes' calls up one response, while the answer 'no' calls up another. With videodisc the machine can respond to your answer by showing an appropriate picture. The diagram on the left gives a simple example.

With a score-keeping facility a tutor can monitor the performance of a student as the responses made are recorded for later reference.

(c) A video player linked to an external computer

This is possible with both videocassette and videodisc players and there are various ways of linking either to a computer. With a separate, independent computer it becomes possible to have a video programme on videodisc or videotape, driven by a computer program on the computer. This means that the same video programme can be driven in different directions by different computer programs. It also means that, with the right equipment, teachers could alter or replace the computer element which in effect does the driving.

The outputs of computer and video can be viewed on separate screens or there are monitors which allow the two to be combined. With the latter it becomes possible to add your own subtitles to a video programme.

This level of interactivity is the most flexible but it is also of course the most expensive and the most complex to use.

Interactive video software

Materials production for this technology is still in its early stages. Some experimental discs are being produced, using conventional video. Brighton Polytechnic Language Centre, with the BBC, is developing interactive videodisc versions of *Bid for Power* and other organisations are also experimenting with ELT and non-ELT materials on videodisc and videocassette. In the United States there has already been some production of material specifically for interactive use, but for most people it is still a question of waiting and seeing what uses, methods and materials emerge.

The major challenge of this development is that it makes it possible to move the emphasis from teaching to learning. Its main potential would seem to lie in its use by individuals working alone or perhaps in small groups, and this requires a very different approach to materials design. Just because the technology offers exciting possibilities, we cannot assume that they will be realised. We can only hope that materials designers will be able to rise to the challenge and that teachers will recognise the role it can play in learning outside the classroom.

11

Making your own materials

This chapter looks at a different kind of self-access — access by teachers to a camera. We discussed in Chapter 7 how a camera might be used in the classroom to record student performance, and in Chapter 9 the recording of teacher performance as part of a teacher-training programme. One other possibility that is sometimes considered if a camera is available in an institution is local production of teaching materials.

English language teaching is a do-it-yourself profession. We can and do make use of all kinds of resources in our own ways: we learn how to draw stickmen and produce our own graphics, we write and record our own audio dialogues, some institutions produce the bulk of their own print materials. It's not surprising then that, if you put a do-it-yourself camera into our hands, the ideas for video production immediately begin to flow. And a video camera is a do-it-yourself tool. It doesn't take long to learn the basics of how to set it up and operate it. The questions you then have to tackle are what you can use it for and, even more important, what you should use it for.

The problem with in-house video production is that any video production, however simple, is time-consuming. It is so time-consuming that you need to look at the end result with a very critical eye and decide whether it was worth the time it took to produce. It is also likely to be unpolished and you need to judge how well it will travel. Would it, for example, stand up to being used by other teachers with other students, possibly even in other institutions?

What can you produce?

The reasons for using video playback in the classroom apply to homemade materials as much as to published materials. A good starting point is to examine your reasons for using video in your own situation. Are there gaps in the materials you have which could be filled by producing something locally? We'll look at possible types of local production, how each can be organised and how each could be used.

Recording someone talking

A very simple way of collecting examples of people talking is to sit them down in front of the camera and get them to talk to it. This kind of material is often referred to as 'talking heads'. Two criticisms are frequently made of it: it is boring and it doesn't exploit the full potential of the medium. But lots of talking-head programmes are very interesting. It all depends on who the heads belong to, what they are talking about and whether we in the audience have a reason for listening to them. As to the second criticism, it is true that a talking-head programme doesn't provide visual clues as to content, but it does permit the language learner to watch as well as listen, to see lip movements and facial expressions and to see what the speaker looks like. All of these factors can in their own way provide visual support to the listening process. Informal research in classrooms has shown that students prefer to see as well as hear a storyteller or lecturer.

The secret of making a good talking-head recording is to find someone who can tell an interesting story. The 'story' could be a description of an experience they have had, a report of an experiment or a piece of fiction. Or you could ask people to give their opinions of a subject on which they have strong views. You can keep the camera work very simple indeed - it can be set to give you the size of picture you want and doesn't need to move. It isn't easy to talk naturally to a piece of machinery and your performers may find it easier to talk to you rather than directly to the camera. Sit as close as you can to one side of the camera and ask them to look at you as they talk. (See page 76 for an illustration of this.)

If you have editing facilities, you could edit together a succession of short 'clips' of different people talking about the same subject. Recordings of different people talking give learners access to a wider range of voices and accents. By making your own recordings you can pick topics and people that are relevant to your own students. You may be able to get someone to talk on a topic that also features in the textbook so that the video recording would introduce listening comprehension work that linked to a reading task. Or you could use a recording as an example of the performance of a task you set the students - the preparation of a report for example.

Recording lectures

Some learners need English in order to be able to follow lectures. Where this is the case, some teachers experiment with ways of collecting examples of lectures and using them as the basis for the language lesson. Audio recordings have been used very successfully for this purpose. If the facilities exist, is it worth making video recordings of a lecture?

Arguments in favour are that the video recording gives a more complete record because it shows what the lecturer writes on the board or displays on the Overhead Projector and it can also cover any demonstrations that are part of the lecture. Linked to this is the way the lecturer refers to what is written on the board or the object of the demonstration - something that may be done verbally or visually. Then there is the whole business of knowing what you are expected to note down and what is intended as a joke, a recycling, or a side issue. This kind of thing is often signalled non-verbally and certainly with students from one cultural tradition coming to study within another culture the non-verbal signals, as well as the verbal, may well be misinterpreted. So the visual record may be very useful in some situations.

Collecting data

In some places it would be possible to use the camera as a 'fly on the wall' to record examples of transactions in the target language in real-life situations relevant to your students. Some examples of what could be set up:

interviews - for jobs
              with the student welfare service
              with the bank manager

buying/selling - shops
                railway station
                theatre

providing services - hotels
                    restaurants
                    information desks

discussions - salesman's visit
              seminar
              any meetings which take place in the target language

All of these are transactions which can be done without asking participants to act in front of the camera. They are situations which could be recorded unobtrusively although you must inform the participants that they will be recorded. They will be conscious of the camera but if this is something they normally do, and if you handle the occasion unobtrusively, allowing some run-in time for everyone to settle down, you can get useable examples of language in action. Your first criterion is relevance to your students: are these the kinds of situations they will have to use the target language in? This relevance makes the material strongly motivating - here is an example of the way *you* will need to use English in a month's time - and therefore the quality of the recording is less important than its immediate relevance.

Recording acted situations

Many institutions make their own audio recordings of dialogues. These are written by teachers and acted by teachers. Often the same is attempted on video but there is a big difference. The fact that you can see as well as hear means that it is much more difficult to make the whole thing credible. With video the setting has to be thought about, the appearance of the characters has to be right and the plain fact of seeing as well as hearing means that it is much more difficult to establish credibility. 'Ham' acting shows up in the slightest twitch of an eyebrow. Professional actors can suggest a character's background and attitude to life in very subtle ways, whereas amateur actors are often just vehicles for the language.

If there is a good argument for producing your own acted scenes with non-actors, try to give them roles similar to their own in real life so that they can play themselves as far as possible. And get someone who has not been involved in the production to give you an honest opinion of the end product.

Evaluating in-house production

Homemade recordings should be judged from two points of view: their viewability and their teachability.

Viewability

It is not easy to set standards for what is acceptable and what is not in terms of production expertise and technical quality. Perhaps the most straightforward questions to ask are: How long will they last? and How far will they travel? Make the analogy with stick-figure drawings: you take more care with something you are going to use over and over again than with something you are going to use in one lesson only. You take more care with something that you are going to show to other people. If you intend to publish in however limited a way then you are more critical of what you are producing. The same is true of a video recording. It doesn't have to have the polish of a broadcast programme if it is not going to be broadcast. On the other hand it has to hold the interest of a class for at least one viewing. Could you send it to another school, to be viewed by people who don't know any of the people who took part in the recording? If the answer is no, does the same apply to other people in your own school using the materials in a year or so when all the participants might be unknown to them? If the answer is still no, then you really need to think hard about how long it took to produce the material and whether that expenditure of time was justified.

Teachability

The main question to ask about any material is: does it do the job it was intended to do with the audience it was made for? Whatever our personal reactions might be to a production, that is the only real test. In order to apply the test it is obviously necessary to get the designers of the material to specify from the beginning what the purpose of the recording is. To decide whether it is successful, we have to know how it was intended to be used and what it was expected to achieve.

Stages of production

Even the simplest recording needs to be planned. These are stages you have to work through and questions you should answer:

1. Make sure it is necessary.
  - What job is the material intended to do?
    (i.e. What are the objectives?)
  - How will the material be used?
  - Why is it necessary to make the material in-house?
  - Why should it be video material?

2. *Spell out the details.*
   - Who is the audience?
   - How will the material fit into a lesson?
   - How long will it be?
   - What resources are needed: people, money, time, equipment, expertise.

3. *Plan the production.*
   - Produce an outline of the programme.
   - Write a script if you need one.
   - Schedule all production dates.
   - Schedule editing time.
   - Fix a deadline for completion.

4. *Produce the material.*

5. *Make sure the material is used.*
   - Will the material be used by others than yourself?
   - Produce notes for other users so that they will understand how you intended to use the material. It is useful to be able to add to these notes as you use the material so that others can benefit from your experience of using it.
   - Be as precise as you can about the role the video recording is intended to have in the teaching programme.
   - How many copies will you need?
   - Let other teachers know it is there - is there a catalogue it should go into?

6. *Evaluate the material.*
   - Try to keep a check on how often it is used and get feedback on how it went.
   - Can you sit in on another teacher using it?
   - How much time did you and others spend on making it?
   - How much classwork does it give you?
   - What reactions does it get from students and other teachers?
   - Does it need revision?
   - Is it worth revising?

Conclusion

We are in an age of rapid technological development. This book has discussed only a few of the innovations we shall have to assess in the next five years or so. There are implications for language teaching and learning in all of them. The distribution of television signals by satellite means that we can have easy access to programmes from other countries in other languages. Cable TV will offer a wide choice of channels and the possibility of calling up what we want when we want it. Computers will be able to produce acceptable speech patterns and they will be able to recognise and react to the human voice. Touch screens will provide another means of interacting with the video/computer screen.

These developments are not usually undertaken with educational applications in mind. It's left to people working in education to discover those applications in their own disciplines. There is a constant need to experiment, to question and to exchange ideas. So we'll finish with some ground rules for assessing new machines and the new materials to go with them.

1. *Talk to other users.*

   The company selling you a new machine should be prepared to give you the names of others who are using it. If they won't that's a danger signal.

   Similarly with new materials, try to find others who have used them, or ask if there are samples available which you could try out.

2. *Assess the machine's properties in the light of your needs.*

   Look at what the machine can do and what you can therefore do with it. Relate this to what you already do in the classroom and decide whether it will help you do any of these things better, save you time, or make the learning process more enjoyable for your students. Don't forget uses by learners outside the classroom.

3. *Allow a trial period.*

   Set a limited period for a trial and establish what you will try out and how you will test the results. Then review your use of the new resource at the end of that period. Remember to ask your students what they thought of it too.

4. *Be prepared for the novelty to wear off.*

   If some of the ideas in this book have been new to you, you may be full of enthusiasm for putting them into practice. This is good. Beware however of overdoing new techniques - you don't have to show everything silently every time, even though it is an exciting technique to use with some video in some classes.

A common pattern when something new is introduced to the classroom, is that there is an initial enthusiasm which then tails off as the new aid becomes a routine element of lessons. Teachers often feel disappointed when student enthusiasm wains. They feel that the new aid has failed, or that they have failed to find the magic touch in using it. But why should an aid be greeted with special enthusiasm after the novelty has worn off? Is it because both teacher and students secretly thought it would make the learning painless, automatic and work-free? If that is the reason then it is quite wrong. The aid is just an aid. It won't take over your teaching and it won't do your students' learning for them. If however you can identify its strengths in your own particular situation then an aid like video could add to the effectiveness of both.

Appendix 1   Published ELT video materials

The materials are listed in alphabetical order by title. The information about each title is drawn mainly from the ELT VIDEO CATALOGUE produced by KELTIC Bookshop, 25 Chepstow Corner, Chepstow Place, London W2 4TT. Tel. 01-229 8560. The catalogue is revised periodically and can be obtained free of charge from the bookshop. Notes on intended use (e.g. broadcast, classroom or self-study) are those indicated by the publisher.

TITLE: The Adventures of Charlie McBride
PUBLISHER: Formavision (only available in France and Spain)
COMPONENTS: video - 180 minutes
 1 C90 audio cassette
 booklet with script, exercises and teacher's notes.
LANGUAGE LEVEL: intermediate
AGE RANGE: secondary/adult

TITLE: At Home in Britain
PUBLISHER: BBC English By Television
COMPONENTS: video - 60 minutes (8 episodes)
 audio cassette
 students' book
 teacher's guide
LANGUAGE LEVEL: intermediate
AGE RANGE: teenager/young adult
DESCRIPTION: Provides examples of British social life. Aimed at young people who come to Britain as students.
For classroom use.

TITLE: The Bellcrest Story
PUBLISHER: BBC English By Television
COMPONENTS: video - 3 hours 15 minutes
 (13 x 15-minute sections)
 audio cassette
 viewer's handbook
 teaching package
LANGUAGE LEVEL: advanced
AGE RANGE: secondary/adult
DESCRIPTION: A serial story about an engineering firm aimed at business people with a good general knowledge of English who need concentration on language relevant to their jobs.
For broadcast or classroom use.

TITLE: Bid for Power
PUBLISHER: BBC English by Television
COMPONENTS: video - 3 hours 15 minutes
 (13 x 15-minute episodes)
 self-instructional) for viewers of
 booklet } the series when
 audio cassette) it is broadcast

 teacher's book)
 students' book } for institutional use
 2 audio cassettes)
LANGUAGE LEVEL: intermediate
AGE RANGE: secondary/adult
DESCRIPTION: A serial story set in the world of international business and industry. Aimed at business people who need to develop their English language skills for business negotiations.
For broadcast or classroom use.
Note: A videodisc version will be published in 1985.

TITLE: The Blind Detective
PUBLISHER: Filmscan Ltd.
COMPONENTS: video - 35 minutes
 (7 x 5-minute stories)
 active viewing guide
 teacher's notes
 workbook
 answer key
 video transcript
LANGUAGE LEVEL: higher intermediate/advanced
AGE RANGE: young adults
DESCRIPTION: Short detective stories set in London.
For self-study or classroom use.

TITLE: Brighton Pictures
PUBLISHER: Mary Glasgow Publications
COMPONENTS: video - 15 minutes
 teacher's notes
LANGUAGE LEVEL: intermediate
AGE RANGE: secondary
DESCRIPTION: Story about the loss of a picture.
For classroom use

TITLE: **Britain Now**
PUBLISHER: **Mary Glasgow Publications**
COMPONENTS: video - 71 minutes (3 videocassettes)
 scripts
LANGUAGE LEVEL: intermediate/advanced
AGE RANGE: secondary
DESCRIPTION: Documentaries about three aspects of British life - roads, sports and animals.
For classroom use.

TITLE: **The British Isles**
PUBLISHER: **Filmscan Ltd.**
COMPONENTS: video - 60 minutes (4 episodes)
 active viewing guide
LANGUAGE LEVEL: intermediate
AGE RANGE: secondary/adult
DESCRIPTION: Cultural background material featuring particular towns and regions in Britain and the people who inhabit them.
For classroom use.

TITLE: **Business**
PUBLISHER: **Filmscan Ltd.**
COMPONENTS: video - 40 minutes (1 videocassette)
 audio cassette (video soundtrack and exercises)
 students' book
LANGUAGE LEVEL: advanced
AGE RANGE: secondary/adult
DESCRIPTION: One of an ESP series for Business and Technical English. Features the offices of the company 3M and presents examples of staff dealing with genuine office situations.
For self-study or classroom use.

TITLE: **Challenges**
PUBLISHER: **BBC English by Television**
COMPONENTS: video - 120 minutes (6 x 20-minute programmes)
 handbook for video
 teaching pack: audio cassettes
 students' book
 teacher's book
 slide set
LANGUAGE LEVEL: advanced
AGE RANGE: secondary/adult
DESCRIPTION: Six documentary programmes feature topics such as work, leisure and love seen through the eyes of young people in contemporary British urban society. The teaching pack forms a multi-media course focussing on idiomatic English used by native speakers.
For classroom use.

TITLE: **Charlie McBride at Home**
PUBLISHER: **Formavision (only available in France and Spain)**
COMPONENTS: video - 100 minutes (2 x 50-minute 'Volumes')
LANGUAGE LEVEL: intermediate
AGE RANGE: secondary/adult
DESCRIPTION: Volume I : 'The Butterfly Hunter'
 Volume II: 'Freedom and the Parrot'
For self-study home use.

TITLE: **Come and See Us**
PUBLISHER: **Filmscan Ltd.**
COMPONENTS: video - 80 minutes
 active viewing guide
LANGUAGE LEVEL: lower intermediate
AGE RANGE: young teenager
DESCRIPTION: Stories based around the adventures of four young people on holiday in the Sussex countryside.
For classroom use.
Note: The publisher suggests that this title combined with 'Double Trouble' and 'Here We Come' provides a supplementary teaching programme for children between the ages of ten and fifteen years.

TITLE: **Comedy Time**
PUBLISHER: **BBC English by Television**
COMPONENTS: video - 120 minutes (4 x 30-minute programmes)
 book of scripts and teaching notes
LANGUAGE LEVEL: near-beginners/lower intermediate
AGE RANGE: secondary/adult
DESCRIPTION: Four comedies, with dialogues written to feature controlled language items. Most of the material is taken from *Follow Me* (see below) where each story appeared as short episodes running through a series of programmes.
For broadcast or classroom use.

TITLE: **Communicate**
PUBLISHER: **Longman Inc.**
COMPONENTS: two videos: Set 1 has 12 lessons;
 Set 2 has eight lessons
 viewer's guide for each level
LANGUAGE LEVEL: Set 1 is for beginners
 Set 2 is for intermediate students
AGE RANGE: secondary/adult
DESCRIPTION: A two-level course with a series of entertaining vignettes depicting real-life situations. The viewer's guides provide a range of interactive and communicative activities.
For classroom use.

TITLE: Double Act
PUBLISHER: Mary Glasgow Publications
COMPONENTS: video - 15 minutes
    teacher's notes
    students' workbook
    audio cassette
    slides
LANGUAGE LEVEL: upper intermediate
AGE RANGE: secondary/young adult
DESCRIPTION: A group of teenagers in a London comprehensive school organise an end-of-term concert.
For classroom use.

TITLE: Double Trouble
PUBLISHER: Filmscan Ltd.
COMPONENTS: video - 80 minutes (8 x 10-minute episodes)
    active viewing guide
    teacher's notes
    workbook
    video transcript
    answer key
LANGUAGE LEVEL: pre-intermediate
AGE RANGE: children, nine years upwards
DESCRIPTION: Situations revolving around three children who form a pop group. Designed to present language.
For self-study or classroom use.

TITLE: Engineering
PUBLISHER: Filmscan Ltd.
COMPONENTS: video - 40 minutes (1 videocassette)
    audio cassette
    students' book
LANGUAGE LEVEL: advanced
AGE RANGE: secondary/adult
DESCRIPTION: One of an ESP series for Business and Technical English. Features engineers in their normal working environment.
For self-study or classroom use.

TITLE: The English Teaching Theatre Video
PUBLISHER: Heinemann
COMPONENTS: video - 30 minutes (1 videocassette)
    links to the language course *Further Off-Stage*
    teacher's book
    students' book
    audio cassette
LANGUAGE LEVEL: students with about two years of English
AGE RANGE: secondary/adult
DESCRIPTION: Video recordings of a selection of the best

sketches performed by the English Teaching Theatre. Each sketch is built around language items commonly found in an EFL syllabus and featured in *Further Off-Stage* so that the video and audio cassettes can be used interchangeably.
For classroom use.

TITLE: Family Affair
PUBLISHER: Longman
COMPONENTS: video - 60 minutes (2 x 30-minute cassettes)
    study guide
    teacher's manual
LANGUAGE LEVEL: elementary to intermediate
AGE RANGE: secondary/adult
DESCRIPTION: A serial story in fifteen episodes in which the language focus follows the same structural and functional syllabus as *Building Strategies*. Can be used to supplement other language coursebooks.
For classroom use.

TITLE: Famous Authors
PUBLISHER: Filmscan Ltd.
COMPONENTS: video - 125 minutes (4 programmes)
    background notes
LANGUAGE LEVEL: advanced
AGE RANGE: adults
DESCRIPTION: An introduction to four literary figures: William Shakespeare, Charles Dickens, D.H.Lawrence, George Orwell.
For classroom or individual use.

TITLE: A Farm in the City
PUBLISHER: Mary Glasgow Publications
COMPONENTS: video - 13 minutes
    audio cassette
    teacher's guide
    workbook
    slides
LANGUAGE LEVEL: students with about two years of English
AGE RANGE: primary
DESCRIPTION: Presents a topic, a community farm in London.
For classroom use.

TITLE: Five Times Britain
PUBLISHER: Filmscan Ltd.
COMPONENTS: video - 100 minutes
    active viewing guide
LANGUAGE LEVEL: upper intermediate
AGE RANGE: secondary/adult
DESCRIPTION: Five documentary programmes about five kinds of British school.
For classroom use.

TITLE: Focus on Britain I and II
PUBLISHER: Mary Glasgow Publications
COMPONENTS: video - 90 minutes (10 x 9-minute
                       programmes on 2 videocassettes)
LANGUAGE LEVEL: lower intermediate/intermediate
AGE RANGE: young adult
DESCRIPTION: Cultural and social background information presented through the story of a young German visitor to Britain. Each part of the story is self-contained so that the material can be used flexibly as a supplement to any main language course.
For classroom use.

TITLE: Follow Me
PUBLISHER: BBC English by Television
COMPONENTS: video - 15 hours (60 x 15-minute
                     programmes)
               4 audio cassettes
               coursebooks
               teacher's guide
LANGUAGE LEVEL: beginner/elementary to threshold level
AGE RANGE: secondary/adult
DESCRIPTION: A two-year course designed to take absolute beginners to threshold level. Based on functional/notional approaches and uses a magazine programme format. Dialogues presenting language items are interspersed with documentary 'spots' and serial story episodes. (See also *Comedy Time* above.)
For broadcast or classroom use.

TITLE: Follow Me to San Francisco
PUBLISHER: BBC English by Television
COMPONENTS: video - 50 minutes (10 x 5-minute
                     episodes)
               students' book
               teacher's manual
LANGUAGE LEVEL: intermediate/upper intermediate
AGE RANGE: secondary/adult
DESCRIPTION: An American English soap opera providing an introduction to language within a North American environment. There is a version with a special commentary available for learners of British English who need to study American English.
For classroom use.

TITLE: Follow Through (in preparation)
PUBLISHER: BBC English by Television
COMPONENTS: video - (15 x 25-minute units)
               textbook
               audio materials
LANGUAGE LEVEL: intermediate
AGE RANGE: late secondary/adult
DESCRIPTION: There are three separate elements in the video component: an entertaining drama series, featuring incidents which present selected language items; a series of short documentaries using authentic and unscripted language, and a thriller serial. Supplementary material is planned.
For broadcast, individual study or classroom use.

TITLE: Framework English
PUBLISHER: Filmscan Ltd.
COMPONENTS: video - 3 hours
               students' workbook
LANGUAGE LEVEL: suitable for all levels
AGE RANGE: adult
DESCRIPTION: A self-study course which concentrates on eight of the major tenses of English by introducing the meaning of the concepts that lie behind them. Can be used by students at different levels.
For self-study use.

TITLE: Hallo
PUBLISHER: Mary Glasgow Publications
COMPONENTS: video - 5 minutes
               coursebooks
LANGUAGE LEVEL: elementary
AGE RANGE: primary
DESCRIPTION: The video sequence shows a boy arriving at school and greeting his friends and teachers. It is linked to the 'Hallo!' course.
For classroom use.

TITLE: Here We Come
PUBLISHER: Filmscan Ltd.
COMPONENTS: video - 60 minutes (5 episodes)
               active viewing guide
LANGUAGE LEVEL: elementary/lower intermediate
AGE RANGE: 12 - 13 years
DESCRIPTION: Adventure stories featuring three English children.
For classroom use.

TITLE: It's Your Turn To Speak
PUBLISHER: Filmscan Ltd.
COMPONENTS: video - 120 minutes (20 lessons)
               students' book
               study guide
LANGUAGE LEVEL: elementary/'false beginners'
AGE RANGE: secondary/adult
DESCRIPTION: Dialogues and some documentary-style sequences present language functions and structures. Video exercises prompt student production of language. British and American English sections.
For self-study or classroom use.

TITLE: Let's Watch

PUBLISHER: Filmscan Ltd.

COMPONENTS: video - 70 minutes (9 units)
audio cassette
students' book
teacher's book

LANGUAGE LEVEL: pre-intermediate/intermediate

AGE RANGE: secondary/adult

DESCRIPTION: Each unit presents a language structure and function within a complete story. The stories centre on everyday events in the lives of two British families. A variety of topics is also introduced in documentary-style sequences. Video-cued exercises and silent viewing sequences provide language practice.

For classroom use. A separate self-study version is also available.

TITLE: Living in Washington

PUBLISHER: Filmscan Ltd.

COMPONENTS: video - 80 minutes (4 episodes)
active viewing guide
teacher's notes
workbook
video transcript
answer key

LANGUAGE LEVEL: intermediate

AGE RANGE: young adults

DESCRIPTION: Cultural and social background on North America. Filmed in the United States, using North American actors and actresses, it centres on three American students. Themes are Leaving Home, Making Friends, First Challenges and Feedback.

For self-study or classroom use.

TITLE: Longman Favourite Fairy Tales

PUBLISHER: Longman

COMPONENTS: video - 60 minutes (2 x 30-minute cassettes covering 6 stories)
6 workbooks with videoscript (1 book for each story)

LANGUAGE LEVEL: post-elementary

AGE RANGE: 7 - 9 years

DESCRIPTION: The six stories (*The Ugly Duckling, The Emperor's New Clothes, The Four Musicians, The Princess and the Pea, Puss in Boots* and *Rapunzel*) are re-told using original full-colour drawings.

For classroom or home use.

TITLE: On We Go

PUBLISHER: BBC English by Television

COMPONENTS: video - 7 hours 30 minutes (30 x 15-minute programmes)
3 audio cassettes
3 students' books
teacher's notes

LANGUAGE LEVEL: elementary/near beginner

AGE RANGE: secondary/young adult

DESCRIPTION: Features language structures within a story about the daily life of four young people in London. Video cues for student listen/repeat.

For broadcast or classroom use.

TITLE: People You Meet

PUBLISHER: BBC English by Television

COMPONENTS: video - 6 hours 30 minutes (26 x 15-minute programmes)
handbook
2 audio cassettes

LANGUAGE LEVEL: intermediate

AGE RANGE: secondary/adult

DESCRIPTION: Each programme is a separate situation comedy which features examples of a particular set of language structures.

For broadcast or classroom use.

TITLE: Person to Person

PUBLISHER: BBC English by Television

COMPONENTS: video - 60 minutes (10 x 6-minute units)
students' book
teacher's manual
audio cassette

LANGUAGE LEVEL: intermediate

AGE RANGE: late secondary/adult

DESCRIPTION: The video covers parts of a day in the life of more than a dozen people in a variety of settings that are likely to be relevant to students. Controlled dialogue presents chosen language functions in operation.

For classroom use.

TITLE: Play and Say

PUBLISHER: Macmillan

COMPONENTS: video - 30 minutes
picture book
play book
video manual for teacher/parent

LANGUAGE LEVEL: beginners

AGE RANGE: kindergarten/juniors

DESCRIPTION: An extension of the course *Play and Say with Paddy and Pip* for young learners of English. The video features the two puppets of the title. Interactive sequences involve children with the doings of the puppets and this is used to present the language and structures of the course.

For home or classroom use.

TITLE: The Sadrina Project
PUBLISHER: BBC English by Television
COMPONENTS: video - 4 hours (12 x 20-minute
    programmes)
    audio cassette
    students' book
    teacher's guide
LANGUAGE LEVEL: intermediate
AGE RANGE: secondary/adult
DESCRIPTION: Features the use of English in travel and the travel business through a serial story. Examples of social and business interactions.
For broadcast and classroom use.

TITLE: Sherlock Holmes and Dr Watson
PUBLISHER: Longman
COMPONENTS: video - 30 minutes (x 8 titles)
    students' workbook
    videoscript
LANGUAGE LEVEL: intermediate
AGE RANGE: secondary/adult
DESCRIPTION: Detective stories, with comprehension exercises built in to the video programme.
For classroom use.

TITLE: Songs Alive
PUBLISHER: BBC English by Television
COMPONENTS: video - 2 hours 30 minutes (10 x
    15-minute programmes)
    audio cassette
    book with words and music of the
    songs, and notes
LANGUAGE LEVEL: intermediate
AGE RANGE: secondary/adult
DESCRIPTION: Songs performed by musicians. Actors illustrate, develop and dramatise the words and stories.
For broadcast or classroom use.

TITLE: Speak Easy
PUBLISHER: BBC English by Television
COMPONENTS: video - 60 minutes (14 sketches)
    audio cassette
    teacher's manual
    students' book
LANGUAGE LEVEL: intermediate
AGE RANGE: secondary/adult
DESCRIPTION: Mime sketches present social encounters and transactions. Several language functions are mimed in the course of each sketch. Designed to lead students to identify the communication needs of the participants and to discover appropriate language. Can be used to teach other languages.
For classroom use.

TITLE: Switch On
PUBLISHER: Filmscan Ltd.
COMPONENTS: video - 60 minutes
    audio cassette
    students' book
    multilingual study notes
    teacher's handbook for class use
LANGUAGE LEVEL: intermediate
AGE RANGE: secondary/adult
DESCRIPTION: A mystery story is used as a vehicle for a course in standard American English. Aimed at people who need remedial English for business trips or conferences.
Mainly self-study but can be used in the classroom.

TITLE: Systems One
PUBLISHER: Language Training Services
COMPONENTS: video - 68 minutes (12 units)
    students' manual
    teacher's manual
LANGUAGE LEVEL: upper intermediate
AGE RANGE: adult
DESCRIPTION: 12 problem-based units with an authentic management training component, based on the management film *What's so special about computers?* Teacher's book covers at least 40 hours of classroom exploitation.
For classroom use.

TITLE: Television English
PUBLISHER: BBC English by Television and the British Council
COMPONENTS: video - 3 hours (6 x 30-minute
    videocassettes)
    teacher's book
LANGUAGE LEVEL: upper intermediate/advanced
AGE RANGE: secondary/adult
DESCRIPTION: Extracts from BBC television archive material selected for use in English Language Teaching. Accompanied by detailed suggestions for use in the classroom. Each videocassette contains six extracts. They will appear singly at about six-monthly intervals.
For classroom use.

TITLE: Travel and Tourism
PUBLISHER: Filmscan Ltd.
COMPONENTS: video - 40 minutes (1 videocassette)
    audio cassette
    students' book
LANGUAGE LEVEL: advanced
AGE RANGE: secondary/adult
DESCRIPTION: One of an ESP series for Business and Technical English. Filmed in the UK offices of

Thomson Holidays and on location in Spain. Features situations arising throughout one particular holiday season.

For self-study or classroom use.

TITLE: Two to Hampstead
PUBLISHER: Mary Glasgow Publications
COMPONENTS: video - 13 minutes
      teacher's notes
LANGUAGE LEVEL: intermediate
AGE RANGE: secondary
DESCRIPTION: An adventure story about two young people who visit Hampstead to discover its history and traditions.

For classroom use.

TITLE: Video English
PUBLISHER: Macmillan and the British Council
COMPONENTS: video - 4 hours (8 x 30-minute videocassettes)
      teacher's notes
      student practice books
LANGUAGE LEVEL: 1 hour each for basic, lower intermediate, upper intermediate and advanced
AGE RANGE: secondary/adult
DESCRIPTION: Elementary (videocassettes 1 and 2) presents and practises basic communicative functions through 48 short scenes; lower intermediate (videocassettes 3 and 4) revises, recycles and extends functions and skills practice in 24 sequences; upper intermediate (videocassettes 5 and 6) presents 12 short stories for viewing comprehension work; advanced level (videocassettes 7 and 8) contains 8 sequences designed to generate debate and discussion.

For classroom use.

TITLE: The Visitor
PUBLISHER: Filmscan Ltd.
COMPONENTS: video - 100 minutes (10 units)
      5 x C40 audio cassettes
      students' book
      activity book
      parent's handbook
      video counter chart
      set of dice and colouring pencils
LANGUAGE LEVEL: beginner
AGE RANGE: children between 9 and 11 years
DESCRIPTION: A space adventure story on video followed by interactive exercises designed to practise and extend new language. Topics covered include home and neighbourhood, entertainment, school and travel, nature and weather and the year. An integrated, multi-media course. Self-study, classroom and other language editions available.

TITLE: Visitron: The Language of Presentations
PUBLISHER: Longman
COMPONENTS: video - 120 minutes (2 x 60-minute cassettes)
      teacher's manual
LANGUAGE LEVEL: intermediate
AGE RANGE: secondary/adult
DESCRIPTION: The course features an independent consultant's presentation to the board of a company which is experiencing severe trading problems. The presentation is then segmented into units which form the basis for intensive classroom work.

For classroom use.

TITLE: We Mean Business
PUBLISHER: Longman
COMPONENTS: video - 60 minutes (14 x 4-minute sketches)
      viewer's handbook
LANGUAGE LEVEL: 'false beginners'/pre-intermediate
AGE RANGE: late secondary/adult
DESCRIPTION: A collection of amusing sketches using the same office situations and language syllabus as the *We Mean Business* coursebook. It can be used as an extension to this course or as a free-standing video-based course.

For classroom use.

TITLE: Your Life In Your Hands
PUBLISHER: Longman Inc.
COMPONENTS: two videos: Level 1 has eight episodes;
      Level 2 has seven episodes
      students' book for each level
      teacher's manual
LANGUAGE LEVEL: Level 1 is for high-beginning students
      Level 2 is for low-intermediate students
AGE RANGE: secondary/adult
DESCRIPTION: This two-level course is a romantic comedy about four young people starting out on their own. Told in 15 episodes, the course covers both functional and structural items. Each episode is preceded by a silent version to prepare students for the sound version.

For classroom use.

Teacher Training Materials

TITLE: Five films for language teachers:

        Activity Days in Language Learning

        Communication Games in a Language
          Programme

        Pair and Group Work in a Language
          Programme

        Using Magazine Pictures in the
          Language Classroom

        Using Tape Recorders in the Language
          Classroom

PUBLISHER: The British Council

COMPONENTS: video - 140 minutes (5 programmes)
          trainer's notes

DESCRIPTION: All five programmes were made in the British Council's English Language Teaching Institute in London and show multi-national classes of adults at different levels. Each programme demonstrates the use of the materials and methods indicated by the title.

TITLE: Teaching Observed

PUBLISHER: BBC English by Television

COMPONENTS: 3 hours 25 minutes (13 x 25-minute
          programmes)
          handbook

DESCRIPTION: Six overseas teachers in 4 countries - Nigeria, Singapore, Sri Lanka and Swaziland - are seen teaching children in their own classrooms. The theme is that the language taught in the classroom must prepare pupils for the language of real life.

Note: The set of teacher training materials entitled *Teaching and Learning in Focus* is referred to and quoted from in Chapter 8. These materials were produced by the British Council to meet its own teacher training needs. For the time being their availability is restricted to British Council centres, apart from those who participated in the project. It is probable that the set will eventually be published in some form.

Appendix 2
Sources of software

Video and Film Sources

BBC English by Radio and Television, PO Box 76, Bush House, London WC2B 4PH (English and EFL Teacher training material)

BBC Enterprises Ltd., Film and Video Sales, Room 503, Villiers House, The Broadway, London W5 2PA *Hire* (UK): Woodston House, Oundle Road, Peterborough PE2 9PZ (French, German, Italian, Spanish and other subjects but not EFL)

Educational Video Index Ltd. 25 Thurloe Street, London SW7 2LH (French and teacher-training films)

Euro-Lang Tapes, 88 Wychwood Avenue, Knowle, Solihull, West Midlands B93 9DQ (English)

Guild Learning, Guild House, Oundle Road, Peterborough PE2 9PZ (English and other subjects)

Language Training Services, 38 Russell Square, London WC1B 5DA (English)

Macmillan Publishers Ltd., Little Essex Street, London WC2R 3LF (English)

Mary Glasgow Publications Ltd., Brookhampton Lane, Kineton, Warwick CV35 0JB (English, French and German)

National Audio Visual Aids Library, Paxton Place, Gipsy Road, London SE27 (English, Chinese, French, German, Hindi, Italian, Russian and Spanish editions of *Hello World*. Also other educational programmes)

Nelson Filmscan, Nelson House, Mayfield Road, Walton on Thames, Surrey KT12 5PL (English)

Materials Lists

THE BRITISH COUNCIL English Language Division Central Information Service *Audio visual aids to English language teaching* (London: British Council, 1980) ETIC information guide 4.
Includes annotated lists of films for ELT and training of language teachers. Also lists other formats.

BRITISH NATIONAL FILM AND VIDEO CATALOGUE (formerly: British National Film Catalogue) Vol. 1 (London: British Film Institute, 1963) Published quarterly with an annual cumulation.
'A record of British and foreign films and videocassettes which have recently been made available for non-theatrical screening in Great Britain.' Lists a wide variety of non-fiction and fiction including (since 1980) feature films. Materials available only for domestic viewing are excluded as are foreign films and videos available for purchase only. Films in various formats and video recordings are listed together in two main sequences. Includes indexes and address lists. Some spin-off publications are also available, including *Films and videograms* for schools.

BUFVC CATALOGUE 1983 (London: British Universities Film and Video Council, 1983) ISBN 0 90129 33 2
Merges and updates *Audio-visual materials for higher education 1979-80 and 1981-82 update* and *Helpis 1982-83*. Annotated list covering various audio-visual formats including film and video. Includes teacher training materials. Published as an A5 booklet with several microfiches. A separate *Distributors index* is also available.

CENTRE FOR INFORMATION ON LANGUAGE TEACHING AND RESEARCH
(a) *Sources of visual and audio aids* (London: CILT, 1982) (Information guides 5a-e). Separate guides for *French, German, Italian, Russian, Spanish*.
Guides include titles of films of cultural interest and addresses of suppliers.
(b) *Teaching materials lists* New series (London: CILT, 1980) The new series provides comprehensive listings with indexes to various formats including film. *French, German* and *Italian* are available now. *Russian* and *Spanish* will be available shortly.

INTER NATIONES
Audiovisuelle Medien: Programm Bonn (Kennedyallee 91-103, D-5300 Bonn 2, West Germany) Annual.
Lists various materials for learning German, available free or at minimal cost to recognised educational institutions. Includes a few videos.

KELTIC *ELT video catalogue* 25 Chepstow Corner, Chepstow Place, London W2 4TT (London: KELTIC Bookshop 1983)
An annotated list, with prices, of videos for

teaching English as a foreign language which were available in July 1983.

NATIONAL ASSOCIATION FOR TEACHING ENGLISH AS A SECOND LANGUAGE TO ADULTS
Films, videos, slides and strips (London: NATESLA, 1983)

An annotated list of materials of interest to teachers of English as a second language in the UK.

NATIONAL VIDEO CLEARINGHOUSE
Penguin Video Source Book (3rd ed.) Harmondsworth, Middlesex (Penguin, 1983) ISBN 014 00 6908 9

Previous editions published as *The Video Source Book — UK* by the National Video Clearinghouse and distributed by Bookwise Video. Provides details of over 7,500 videos available in the UK. Wide general coverage including feature films, children's programmes, sport, science, business, industry and education. Mainly English language material but versions in other languages are indicated when available.

Appendix 3
Further reading

Video in English Language Teaching

BBC ENGLISH BY TELEVISION *Using Video in the Classroom* (1981)

BEVAN,V, LASCHE,S and SCHWARTZ,J *An Intensive Theme-Oriented Course in Advanced English for First-Semester German University Students of Diverse Subject Studies* (Free University of Berlin)

CANDLIN,J, CHARLES,D and WILLIS,J *Video in English Language Teaching* (A Language Studies Unit Research Report, University of Aston in Birmingham 1982)

GEDDES,M and STURTRIDGE,G (eds.) *Video in the Language Classroom* (Heinemann 1982)

LAVERY,M, O'BRIEN,T and REVELL,J *Active Viewing Plus* (Modern English Publications 1983)

LONERGAN,J *Video in Language Teaching* (Cambridge University Press 1984)

McGOVERN,J (ed) *Video Applications in English Language Teaching* (Pergamon Press in association with The British Council 1983)

RILEY,P Viewing Comprehension: "L'oeuil ecoute" in *The Teaching of Listening Comprehension* (ELT Documents Special. The British Council 1979)

TOMALIN,B *Using Video, TV and Radio in the Classroom.* (Macmillan 1984)

Non-verbal communication

BIRDWHISTELL,R L *Kinesics and Context* (University of Pennsylvania Press 1970)

HINDE,R A (ed.) *Non-Verbal Communication* (Cambridge University Press 1972)

LAVER,J and HUTCHESON,S *Communication in Face to Face Interaction* (Penguin 1972)

General: video and television

ATIENZA,L J *VTR Workshop: a small format guide* (Paris: Unesco 1977: distributed by Centre for Advanced TV Studies, London)

COMBES,P and TIFFIN,J *Television Production for Education* (Focal Press 1978)

CRABB,G *Copyright clearance: a practical guide* (London 1977: Council for Educational Technology)

MOSS,R *Video: The Educational Challenge* (Croom Helm 1983)

PARSLOE,E (ed.) *Interactive Video* (Sigma Technical Press 1983)

ROWATT,R W *Video: a guide to the use of portable video equipment* (Glasgow: Scottish Council for Educational Technology 1980)

SHERRINGTON,R *Television and Language Skills* (Oxford University Press 1973)

Index of techniques